If you're content with [...] "Christianity," or if yo[...] siren call of the world [...] trouble-free, self-cente[...] if you're hungry for more of God; if you long to rise above the pull and distractions of our culture and enter into all for which God created and saved you; if you want to live a life that outlasts you; and if you want to experience the sweet fruit of true love, sacrifice, holiness, and courage, then I urge you to read *The Set-Apart Woman*. Let it rock your world and let it challenge you to build your life on the Rock, Christ Jesus.

NANCY LEIGH DEMOSS
Author and *Revive Our Hearts* teacher and host

If you want to be entertained or pampered as a Christian reader, do not read this book! But if you really love Jesus Christ and desire more than anything to become the person He created you to be, this book is for you! In *The Set-Apart Woman*, Leslie Ludy pours out her heart, calling us to leave behind the "rags" of current pop culture in order to become a beautiful woman clothed with the likeness of Jesus Christ. I could hardly put the book down as my own life was challenged! (Every Christian needs to take a hard look at the subtle, devious ways the world has crept into one's everyday life.)

Leslie's open and honest sharing of her own struggle connects us to reality. Her balanced teaching on what it means to be transformed by Jesus Himself rather than legalistic religion is refreshing. Her strong stand on biblical principle is convincing! The life that Leslie describes would be impossible were it not for Jesus—*His very life* alive in the heart of every Christian who is ready and willing to exchange all broken self-centeredness for all that He is. Want it? God has spoken into the life of Leslie Ludy, and we who long to love the Lord our God with all our hearts would do well to listen as she speaks into our lives through the pages of this book!

BONNIE BARROWS THOMAS
Torchbearers International

THE
Set-apart WOMAN

GOD'S INVITATION TO SACRED LIVING

LESLIE LUDY

A NavPress resource published in alliance
with Tyndale House Publishers, Inc.

NavPress is the publishing ministry of The Navigators, an international Christian organization and leader in personal spiritual development. NavPress is committed to helping people grow spiritually and enjoy lives of meaning and hope through personal and group resources that are biblically rooted, culturally relevant, and highly practical.

For more information, visit www.NavPress.com.

Library of Congress Cataloging-in-Publication Data
Ludy, Leslie.
  The set-apart woman : God's invitation to sacred living / Leslie Ludy.
    pages cm
  Includes bibliographical references.
  ISBN 978-1-61291-825-9
1. Christian women—Religious life. 2. Christian women—Conduct of life. I. Title.
  BV4527′L84 2015
  248.8′43—dc23   2014048053

Printed in the United States of America

24   23   22
8   7   6   5

TABLE OF CONTENTS

But know that the LORD has
set apart the godly for himself.

PSALM 4:3, ESV

CHAPTER ONE

The Divine Invitation

The Sacred Call to Come Away with Jesus

Come out from among them and be separate, says the Lord.
Do not touch what is unclean, and I will receive you.

2 CORINTHIANS 6:17

My beloved spoke, and said to me:
"Rise up, my love, my fair one, and come away."

SONG OF SOLOMON 2:10

He who hath given himself entirely unto God,
will never think he doth too much for Him.

HENRY SCOUGAL, *The Life of God in the Soul of Man*

Comrades in this solemn fight . . . let us settle it as something that
cannot be shaken: we are here to live holy, loving, lowly lives.
We cannot do this unless we walk very, very close to our Lord Jesus.
Anything that would hinder us from the closest walk possible to us
till we see Him face to face is not for us.

AMY CARMICHAEL, *God's Missionary*

I T WAS A BALMY Sunday night about ten years ago. Eric and I were preparing to speak at the evening service of a large church, sitting in the greenroom with the worship team as they waited for their turn to go onstage. I sipped from a bottle of water and listened to the lighthearted banter that swirled around us.

The guitar player had just been to an exciting play-off game and was giving the associate pastor an animated description of all the action. The drummer was inviting the bass player over after church to try out his new Xbox. The worship leader was sharing his artistic analysis of the Hollywood blockbuster he'd just seen with one of the tech guys.

"Hey, did anyone watch *Saturday Night Live* last night?" the keyboard player suddenly asked.

"Oh, yeah!" the guitar player responded. "It was hilarious, man!"

The worship leader quickly chimed in with, "I was laughing so hard I had Pepsi coming out of my nose!"

For the next five minutes, the group relived the comedic antics of their favorite actors on the show, repeating all the crude and sarcastic one-liners verbatim. They carried on until the worship leader finally said, "Okay, guys, let's get serious. We're starting in a minute. Who wants to pray?"

Like a light switching off, the joking abruptly ceased as everyone huddled together for prayer. Someone offered a short petition for God to be glorified in the service. After a corporate "amen" they hurried to take their positions onstage.

Eric and I watched as they led the congregation in worship, closing their eyes and lifting their hands to heaven dramatically as they sang.

I felt uncomfortable as I observed the scene. How could these Christians go straight from reveling in the ungodly humor of *Saturday Night Live* into a worship session in which they claimed Christ as their "all in all"? But I soon realized that my inner discomfort wasn't merely from watching the worship team's double standard; it was also from the prick of my own conscience.

You have the same compromise in your own life, an inner Voice reminded me gently.

I bristled in self-defense. Sure, I too was a Christian leader who sometimes got preoccupied with pop culture. But at least I put some space in between my worldly indulgences and my ministry life. And I was at least somewhat careful about what I watched and listened to. Compared to a lot of what I saw in modern Christianity, my life seemed pure and Christ-centered. And yet . . .

Come away with Me, and leave mediocrity and compromise behind, the beckoning Voice spoke to my heart. *You had something more than this once, and you have let it slip away.*

I was reminded of that season years ago when, as a young woman, I surrendered my life to Jesus Christ. As I had let go of sinful patterns and yielded to the refining work of God's Spirit, He had gently purged my life of worldly mentalities and ungodly habits. He had taught me how to build my life around Him rather than merely fit Him into my life. He had shaped me into a set-apart young woman. I no longer chased after the shallow distractions of pop culture. He became the delight of my heart—not just in word, but in day-to-day reality.

But now, so many years later, something had changed. I still had a semblance of intimacy with Christ. I was still having daily quiet times and reading my Bible. I was still living morally and speaking Truth. My testimony continued to inspire and strengthen other believers. But until this moment, I hadn't realized that my spiritual life had grown dull, my relationship with Christ had grown distant, and I had become preoccupied with the distractions of the world.

My heart ached with the clear revelation that I had left my first love, just like the church of Ephesus in the book of Revelation (2:4). I'd been so busy getting ruffled over the compromise and worldliness in the lives of Christians around me that I hadn't noticed that I was guilty of many of the same pitfalls.

During the early years of my relationship with Christ, I had understood what it meant to be consecrated to Him. Instead of spending time on frivolity, I had spent time in prayer and the Word of God. Instead of chasing after popularity, I had learned how to put others first and serve those in need. In our premarriage days, Eric and I had spent the majority of our time on eternal things, not temporal ones. We weren't consumed with pop culture, but with learning more about God and growing closer to Him. We'd studied Christian biographies and gleaned wisdom from the lives of great men and women who had gone before us. Scripture was alive and powerful. Our spiritual fire had burned bright and strong.

But as we grew older and became Christian influencers, the pressures of leadership started taking their toll. Public ministry was grueling, and we often found ourselves drawn to pop-culture entertainment to find our reprieve. We felt entitled to a break from being in "ministry-leader mode" all the time, and believed it was our responsibility to stay in touch with the culture by being "clued in" to society's trends in music, media, and professional sports. We felt we were spiritually mature enough to separate the good from the bad. We didn't think a few worldly pastimes would harm us, as long as we were careful to put reasonable boundaries around what we listened to and watched.

None of the Christian leaders I knew would have expressed concern over these activities. They themselves regularly participated in the same things. In fact, more than one respected Christian had advised Eric and me to engage in these pastimes as a way to decompress from the pressures of being in public ministry.

"You can't be spiritual *all* the time," one pastor friend had told us, "otherwise you'll just burn yourself out."

Those seemed like wise words. We lived a demanding life. What was wrong with escaping every now and then and enjoying the pleasures of pop culture for a while (within reasonable Christian boundaries, of course)? But as I evaluated our lifestyle in light of the set-apartness and spiritual passion we'd once had, I knew I had lost something sacred. I still believed all the same things. But my spiritual fire had faded to a flicker. I had lost my hunger for more of God. I realized I was guilty of the same hypocrisy as those worshipers onstage: honoring Christ with my mouth but not with my heart and life. I had to admit that I would rather spend an evening curled up on the couch in front of the T.V. than on my knees in prayer or studying God's Word. I felt more at home surfing the Internet for new fashion trends than searching the Word of God for priceless nuggets of Truth. And I was far more inclined to open a Grisham novel than an inspiring Christian biography.

The more comfortable I had become with the world's messages, the easier it had become to allow subtle sins into my life. Self-pity, laziness, and selfishness had become familiar companions, along with many other "small" compromises. Because they had crept in gradually, it was easy to excuse them and allow them to remain.

I felt convicted and ashamed as I realized how far from the center I had strayed, even as a Christian leader. I had traded spiritual passion for mediocrity. I was loving Christ with only part of my heart, rather than with my entire being.

God's message to my soul was unmistakable: "Remember from where you have fallen, and repent and do the deeds you did at first" (Rev. 2:5, NASB). He was asking me to rise up and come away with Him—to exchange mediocrity, compromise, and worldliness for something infinitely more beautiful and fulfilling: unhindered fellowship with Jesus Christ. He was reminding me of the consecrated, Christ-centered life I was called to live. He was ready to purify me from the inside out and ignite my spiritual fire once again.

For several years, I had been disturbed over the mediocrity I had seen in the modern church. I'd prayed many times for revival to sweep over American Christianity. But now I saw that I needed a personal revival before I'd be ready to pray for a corporate one. *Lord, send a revival, and let it begin in my own soul!* was the resounding cry of my heart as I left the church that evening.

Over the following months and into the next couple years, a profound transformation took place within my soul. Eric was walking through a similar awakening, and we began to talk for hours about what God was doing within each of us. We repented of the worldliness and compromise we'd yielded to. We allowed God's Spirit to shine His searchlight deep within our souls and purge away the dross of selfishness and sinful habits. We became broken over our sin and hungry for His righteousness. The worldly pastimes that had once seemed so important now held no attraction to either of us. We pressed into God with more fervency than we ever had before, even in the early days of our conversions.

That revival season became a turning point in our Christian lives. We began to understand the power and fullness of the Gospel for the first time. It's not that what we'd had previously wasn't genuine Christianity. But it was incomplete. Much like a house with plumbing or electricity that had never been hooked up, we'd had something real and tangible, but it had never functioned at its full potential.

We asked God to show us how to keep our spiritual fire from fading and compromise from creeping back in. We asked Him to give us a single-minded, unshakable loyalty to Him. As we embraced a life of wholehearted consecration to Jesus Christ, we began to experience a vibrant, victorious Christianity that permeated every area of our existence.

This wasn't just a spiritual high. The change was a lasting one. The victory, joy, peace, and intimacy with Christ that we discovered during that time have remained strong, deepening and growing ever since—even through some of the most intense trials we've ever experienced.

Yes, we have had struggles and failures along the way. And we have certainly not "arrived" in our journey toward complete consecration to Jesus Christ. There are always new areas in which He must gently convict us of sin and deepen our understanding of what it means to be set apart for Him. But by His grace, we gained something during that season that has transformed our Christian existence—an unshakable passion for Jesus Christ. Our spiritual flicker became a steady, burning flame when we stopped pining after the things of this world and started pining after Him instead.

A HOLY DISCONTENT

Have you ever felt a longing for *something more* in your relationship with Jesus Christ?

Maybe you have picked up this book because you feel a holy discontent within your soul: that persistent, gentle tug of Christ's Spirit, asking you to come away with Him; to leave mediocrity and compromise behind; to become fully, wholly, completely *His*; to love Him *radically*—not merely with your words, but with your entire heart, soul, mind, and strength. Maybe you are growing dissatisfied with mediocrity, and you long to live a life of passionate devotion to the one true King, but you aren't sure how.

The Bible describes a time when the people of Israel had to make a choice about which king they would serve—David or Saul. Though David was God's chosen king for Israel, he had been forced to run for his life and was reduced to living in a cave. Saul was still in control of the kingdom. He was obsessed with finding and killing David, and anyone showing loyalty to the cave-dwelling outlaw would be guilty of treason and put to death.

Those who were willing to remain under Saul's rule could enjoy an easy, comfortable life, free from persecution and hardship. But there were some who refused to choose their own comfort over loyalty to the one true king. They had become dissatisfied serving a selfish king. They knew that choosing to serve David would mean leaving their security and comforts behind and choosing a life of difficulty over a life of ease. To join David in the cave meant living in exile, having a rock for a pillow, and being on Saul's most-wanted list. Yet these men were so discontent living under Saul's control that they became willing to give up their very lives in order to serve the one true king. So they made the courageous choice to go to David and pledge their lives to his service (see 1 Sam. 22:2).

When these brave men left Saul's camp to dwell in the lowly cave with the true king, their lives were not comfortable or easy. They were hunted and hated, just as David was. They took on David's reproach and became known as traitors, just like he was. And yet they developed such a deep, unshakable love and loyalty to their king that nothing else mattered but serving and honoring him. David's name means "beloved," and his followers treated him as such. They knew that, even with all its risks and hardships, serving David was the most fulfilling and amazing life they could ever choose.

David's men powerfully demonstrated their incredible love and loyalty toward him during an event that took place during David's exile in the cave. The Philistines had taken control of much of Israel, and the soldiers were holding hostage the town of Bethlehem, the place of David's birth. Parched with thirst, David expressed his longing for a sip of water from a certain well in Bethlehem: "Oh, that someone would give me a drink of water from the well of Bethlehem, which is by the gate!" (1 Chron. 11:17).

It would have been a death mission for David to send any of his men to the well, which was surrounded by enemy soldiers. His statement had merely been wishful thinking: "If only it were possible for me to quench my thirst with a drink from that well!"

But David's men lived for only one purpose—to serve and honor God's anointed king. Upon hearing his desire for water from that well, three of his men sprang into action.

If their king wanted a drink from the well, then they were determined to get it for him at any cost.

> So the three broke through the camp of the Philistines, drew water from the well of Bethlehem that was by the gate, and took it and brought it to David. Nevertheless David would not drink it, but poured it out to the LORD. And he said, "Far be it from me, O my God, that I should do this! Shall I drink the blood of these men who have put their lives in jeopardy? For at the risk of their lives they brought it."
>
> (1 CHRON. 11:18-19)

Their awe-inspiring example begs the question: *Do we possess that kind of to-the-death loyalty to our true King, Jesus Christ?* Are we so radically devoted to Him that we will gladly exchange the comforts of Saul's kingdom for the difficulties and dangers of David's cave? Do we love Him so much that we will become numbered among the hunted and despised along with Him? Are we willing to charge straight into the most deadly peril, at risk of our own lives, simply to honor His slightest request?

These questions challenge me at the deepest level of my soul.

There have been all too many times in my life when I have been guilty of "drawing near to Him with my mouth and honoring Him with my lips, while my heart was far from Him" (see Mt. 15:8). There have been too many times when my own security and comfort mattered more than bringing glory to His name.

Perhaps you can relate.

Many of us are happy to sing songs about Christ, write about Him, and talk about Him to other believers, but often when the true test of loyalty comes, we choose personal comfort over radical abandon to Him. We might take a few small risks for our King, but if He asked for a drink from a well that was surrounded by enemy warriors, we'd reason, *If I went that far in my devotion to Him, I'd be putting myself at risk. I'd be making myself vulnerable to discomfort and pain. I might even get killed. I can't give up everything for Him; it's just not reasonable!*

But Jesus Christ gave up everything for us. And He is asking if we will give Him everything in return. Saying a wholehearted yes to this priceless opportunity is the secret to discovering the vibrant, victorious Christianity of the Bible and finding that *something more* our hearts are longing for.

In recent years, I have had the privilege of meeting many men and women who are consecrated to Jesus Christ. They have been set free from worldliness, sinful strongholds, and mediocrity. They are living lives of radical abandon to Him. Many have given up comforts, material possessions, security, fame, position, and personal pursuits in order to take up their cross and follow Him (see Mt. 16:24). But even though they have lost so many things that this world deems important, they are some of the happiest, most content, and most self-sacrificing people anywhere.

Why? Because they have forsaken compromise and medi-ocrity and come away with Jesus. He has become their *every-thing*, not just in their words, but in their day-to-day reality.

Are they perfect? Of course not. They are continually being refined and corrected by God's Spirit, as we all are. But the spiritual victory and vibrant intimacy with Jesus Christ they have discovered is *real*, and it is *lasting*.

Do they have struggles? Of course. But by God's grace, they have learned to triumph through trials, to fight the Enemy's harassments with prayer, and to overcome his lies with Truth.

Just as David's men forsook their allegiance to Saul, these men and women have cut off their allegiance to this world. They are not preoccupied with pop culture. They would much rather spend an hour at the feet of Jesus than watching the latest comedy on T.V. They have built their lives around the eternal rather than the temporal. They have a joy that cannot be shaken, even during the most severe trials. Because of their single-minded, passionate, unwavering loyalty to the one true King, and their willingness to follow Him with radi-cal abandon, they have discovered a Christianity that *really works*. And their lives are profoundly, eternally impacting this world as a result.

THE INVITATION

Do you desire to *know* Jesus Christ deeply and intimately, as your dearest, closest, most trusted Friend? Do you long to not just talk about Him, sing about Him, and learn about

Him, but to truly walk in daily, passionate relationship with Him? Are you tired of just reading about God's promises in the Bible and ready to *actually experience* the unmatched joy, peace that passes understanding, and soul-level satisfaction that is promised to those who follow Him?

If that is the kind of Christianity that you long for, this book is an invitation to forsake the comforts and security of Saul's camp and come away to the cave with your Beloved. From the outside, the cave may appear to be the most undesirable place in the world. Because when you choose to go where He is, you must also choose to give up your life as you know it and become numbered among the hunted and despised. Going where He is may even cost your very life.

But when you are in intimate fellowship with the true King, all of the risks and discomforts pale in comparison to the sheer wonder and joy of abiding in His presence. When you truly come away with Jesus, you won't focus on what you are giving up, but on what you are gaining. Your love for Him will become so great that the cry of your heart will echo the words of the Waldensian martyr from the Middle Ages who, at the time of his death, declared, "Ten thousand deaths would be too few to express my love for Him!"

There is more to Christianity than what most of us are experiencing today. There is more to intimacy with Jesus Christ than what most of us have discovered. There is more to being a believer in Jesus than adopting a few Christian morals and being part of a "Christian social club" called church. There is more to the Christian life than what many leaders today are preaching.

Yes, I know that not everyone appreciates hearing that "there is more," because it implies that we must change—that we as modern Christians are not where we are supposed to be. It means we can't live in mediocrity while giving lip service to Christ. To come away with our true King, we cannot just visit the cave from time to time. We must *abide* there. To become a loyal servant of David, there can be no allegiance to Saul. To be a true follower of Jesus, there can be no turning back.

Over the past twenty years in Christian ministry, I have encountered two kinds of believers. There are those who are content to remain comfortably where they are, and there are those who have a holy discontent—a longing for something deeper. If you are one of the latter group, you are dissatisfied with just going through the motions of Christianity. You want the real thing. You don't want to merely draw near to Christ with your words; you desire a real, passionate, daily relationship with Him. You want to experience the joy, peace, victory, faith, and power promised in Scripture to those who believe. You want the kind of to-the-death loyalty to Jesus Christ that David's "mighty ones" had for their king.

If that describes you, read on! This message won't tickle your ears, but it *will* stir and awaken your soul. And, Lord willing, it will help you discover the *something more* in your Christianity that you have been longing for.

Let me say it up front: This book presents a challenging message. While my writing style is not fire and brimstone, it also isn't fluff and feel-good. There are plenty of books out there that will let you stay comfortably where you are; this is not one of them. This message is meant to take you somewhere, to push you to greater depths of intimacy with Christ and pull you toward greater heights of spiritual triumph. This book will call you to become a set-apart woman, to exchange sin and mediocrity for a set-apart, Christ-consumed life. It's an exciting journey, but it's not an easy one.

As Christian women, our preferences hold a lot of influence over the kinds of books, music, and messages that are impacting the church today. We are the main purchasers of Christian products and the biggest participants in Christian events. I've heard many leaders declare that today's Christian women are too emotionally delicate to be challenged with serious Gospel truth or too busy and distracted to digest messages with deep spiritual substance. Thus, the church is overflowing with shallow Christian fluff that waters down the Gospel and leaves us spiritually empty.

What if we as Christian women got *serious* about our pursuit of Jesus Christ? What if we became broken over our sin, desperate for undiluted Truth, and willing to radically follow Him with all our heart, soul, mind, and strength? Imagine how modern Christianity could change. (I do not discount the important role of men in the Body of Christ. But this book was written primarily for today's Christian women so that is where my emphasis is.)

It is my prayer that this book will point you toward that end. It is my desire to not only cast an inspiring and beautiful vision for biblical, Christ-centered, set-apart womanhood, but also to equip you to live it out. I'll be honest about the struggles and victories I've faced in my own pursuit to become a set-apart woman and share specific ways that God has challenged me with the truths presented in this book.

I hope that this message helps you see Jesus more clearly and know Him more intimately. May it become a catalyst for God's refining fire to purify your heart and life, so that you can become a powerful instrument of change in the Body of Christ today.

Lord, send a revival, and let it begin in us!

If we want to have unhindered fellowship with Jesus, we must be willing to come away from anything and everything standing in the way of wholehearted consecration to Him. Jesus stands ready to take your hand and lead you away from the empty pursuits of this world into the glorious realities of His kingdom. He is inviting you to "rise up . . . and come away" with Him (see S. of S. 2:10). He desires to set you apart for His purposes and for His glory.

Jeremiah 29:13 says, "You will seek Me and find Me, when you search for Me with *all* your heart" (emphasis added). When our desire for Christ becomes so great that

we begin to seek Him as if we are searching for priceless treasure (see Ps. 119:72), when we are willing to give up all the
treasures of this world in order to gain Him (see Mt. 13:46;
Phil. 3:8)—that is when He will draw nearer to us than we
ever imagined possible. Charles Spurgeon wrote,

> Jesus says, "Rise up, My love, My fair one and
> come away." He asks you to come out from the
> world and be separate and touch not the unclean
> thing. . . . Come altogether away from selfishness—
> from anything which would divide your chaste
> and pure love to Christ—your soul's Husband. . . .
> Come away from your old habits. . . Leave all these
> things. . . . Come away to private communion. . . .
> Come away, shut the doors of your chamber
> and talk with your Lord Jesus and have close
> and intimate dealing with Him . . . [Come]
> right away from the world . . . by making
> your dedication to Christ perfect, complete,
> unreserved, sincere, spotless.[1]

Are you ready to come away with your true King?

LET'S TALK ABOUT IT

Group Study and Discussion

1. **READ LUKE 14:27,33.** What does it mean to be a disciple of Jesus Christ? How does this standard differ from the version of Christianity that many of us adopt?

2. **READ SONG OF SOLOMON 2:10.** What does it mean to rise up and come away with Jesus? When we accept this invitation, how do our lives change?

TAKE IT DEEPER

Personal Study and Reflection

READ: 1 SAMUEL 22:2

REFLECT: Do I have a holy discontent toward mediocre Christianity? Am I willing to pursue something deeper by forsaking the comfort and ease of Saul's camp in order to serve David in the humble cave? What would that look like in my daily life?

READ: PSALM 45:10-11

REFLECT: Do I sense Christ calling me to come away with Him? Am I willing to serve Him without holding back, and offer myself completely to Him without reserve? (If yes, take some time to consecrate your life to Him. If no, ask Him to make your heart willing to take this radical step of obedience.)

CHAPTER TWO

Clinging to the Cross

The Secret to Set-Apartness

*By faith Moses . . . [chose] rather to suffer affliction with the
people of God than to enjoy the passing pleasures of sin, esteeming
the reproach of Christ greater riches than the treasures in Egypt;
for he looked to the reward.*

HEBREWS 11:24-26

*I determined not to know anything among you except Jesus Christ
and Him crucified.*

1 CORINTHIANS 2:2

*Why should a person come to the cross? Why should a person embrace
death with Christ? . . . I'll tell you why! Because it's the only way
that God can get glory out of a human being!*

PARIS REIDHEAD, "Ten Shekels and a Shirt"

*I will cherish the old rugged cross, till my trophies at last I lay down;
I will cling to the old rugged cross, and exchange it someday for
a crown. // O that old rugged cross, so despised by the world,
has a wondrous attraction for me; // for the dear Lamb of God
left His glory above to bear it to dark Calvary. // To that old
rugged cross I will ever be true, its shame and reproach gladly
bear; // Then He'll call me someday to my home far away,
where His glory forever I'll share.*

GEORGE BENNARD, "The Old Rugged Cross"

W HEN ERIC WAS in his early twenties, he went on a mission trip to inner-city New Orleans near the time of Mardi Gras. One night his team decided to do street evangelism on Bourbon Street, holding up a large wooden cross as they preached and handed out tracts. Eric was new to street evangelism and reluctant to participate. He felt there were better ways to share the Gospel, ways that wouldn't make him look like a fool. As the other missionaries set up the large wooden cross amid a sea of drunken partiers, Eric kept his distance.

As long as he remained a safe distance away from the cross, he could pretend that he wasn't really with those "kooky Christians" who were preaching about Jesus amid a mocking crowd. He stood there awkwardly, halfway between the swarm of noisy street revelers and the group of missionaries with the wooden cross. Though his heart was pounding and his body tense, he tried to look as nonchalant as possible. *Maybe I can just hang in the background and silently pray for these lost souls*, he reasoned.

But he was so uncomfortable he couldn't even put two words together for a prayer. All he could think about was how to stand as far away from the cross as possible without abandoning his missionary team. He didn't want to be part of the wild street crowd. But he also didn't want to be part of the radical team of missionaries who were being ridiculed and scorned by everyone around them. So he remained halfway between the two, feeling miserable.

"Hey, Eric!" One of his team members motioned to him. "Can you come here and hold up the cross?"

He froze on the spot. He'd been trying to stay away from the wooden cross. How could he swallow his pride enough to hold it up in the middle of Bourbon Street?

Despite his hesitation, he suddenly found himself walking toward the wooden cross and placing his hand on it. The moment that he grabbed on to the cross and faced the partiers, he felt a strange emotion overtake him. Pure joy. A sense of radiant happiness flooded through him, and he couldn't keep a smile from spreading across his face. Just a few minutes earlier, he'd been safe from public mockery, but he was restless and miserable. Now, though the object of ridicule, he felt excited and alive.

As Eric held on to the cross, he pondered the dramatic transformation that had taken place within his soul. There was no longer any question where he stood. He had crossed the line and chosen his side. Everyone who saw him knew he was with Jesus. They laughed, they cursed, they spit, and they threw beer. They hated him because of the cross that he was holding—and he'd never been happier. As he clung to the cross, only one thing seemed important: standing boldly for the glory of his precious King.

An hour later when another missionary asked for a turn holding the cross, Eric reluctantly handed it off. He would have held that cross all night if he'd been able to. He had stumbled upon the secret to vibrant Christianity: not merely standing *near* the Cross, but *clinging* to it and gladly bearing its reproach.

FORSAKING MEDIOCRITY

As you consider what it means to be set apart for Christ, you must examine your life in light of a crucial question: Are you standing in the *vicinity* of the Cross, or are you *clinging* to it? Are you constantly strategizing how to stand as far away from Christ as possible, while still calling yourself a Christian? Is your own reputation more important to you than His?

The author of Hebrews described how Moses willingly chose to forgo the prestige and ease of Pharaoh's palace, choosing to embrace the reproach of Christ rather than to "enjoy the passing pleasures of sin" (vv. 24-26).

Are we willing to make that same exchange?

Amy Carmichael, a missionary to India in the late 1800s, wrote, "Ours should be the love that asks not, 'How little?' but 'How much?'; the love that pours out its all and revels in the joy of having anything to pour on the feet of its Beloved."[1]

How can we avoid mediocre Christianity? We must stop waffling somewhere between the world and the Cross. Many of us embrace Christianity only so far as it does not threaten our comforts or popularity. But true set-apartness means clinging to the Cross and lifting it high for the world to see. It means living in such a way that leaves no questions as to where our true loyalties lie. When people observe our lives, they should see us unashamedly embracing the Cross and boldly declaring, "I'm with Him!"

WHAT WILL REALLY CHANGE THE WORLD?

A well-known pastor has several framed photos in his office, showing him standing next to various famous athletes and movie stars, most of whom openly live immoral lives.

A popular Christian radio station proudly announced that one of their favorite Christian artists recently got to open for a famous (and very ungodly) rock star.

When Hollywood and the secular music industry feel comfortable with us (and we feel comfortable with them), something is wrong with our Christianity. Yet more and more Christians are accepting the idea that the more attractive we are to the culture, the better witnesses we will be.

A couple of years ago I spoke at a women's event on set-apartness, and many of the women were deeply stirred by the message of "coming away" from worldliness and being consecrated to Christ. But one of the leaders was uncomfortable. "What you are sharing is too extreme," she told me during one of the breaks. "We teach women that in order to become the fragrance of Christ they cannot be fortressed in from the world. They must become part of the culture in order to reach it."

But Jesus said something quite different. "If the world hates you, you know that it hated Me before it hated you. If you were of the world, the world would love its own. Yet because you are not of the world, but I chose you out of the world, therefore the world hates you" (Jn. 15:18-19). And,

"Woe to you when all men speak well of you, for so did their fathers to the false prophets" (Lk. 6:26).

True Christianity will influence the world, but it will never be applauded by the world. Catherine Booth, the cofounder of the Salvation Army, wrote:

> When the Church and the world can jog
> comfortably together, you may be sure there is
> something wrong. The world has not altered.
> Its spirit is exactly the same as it ever was, and if
> Christians were equally faithful and devoted to
> the Lord, and separated from the world, living so
> that their lives were a reproof to all ungodliness,
> the world would hate them as much as it ever did.[2]

True Christianity has always been, and will always be, offensive to the culture. And only when we no longer care what we look like to this world can we truly impact it for Jesus Christ.

So what does it mean to become the "fragrance of Christ" to this lost and dying world? Let's take a closer look at what Scripture says: "For we are to God the pleasing aroma of Christ among those who are being saved and those who are perishing. To the one we are an aroma that brings death; to the other, an aroma that brings life" (2 Cor. 2:15-16, NIV).

God says that our lives will give off an appealing fragrance to those who are ready to receive Christ, but to those enslaved to sin, our separation from the world will cause offense everywhere we go. There is no way around it. We have fooled ourselves if we think that worldliness somehow brings glory to God. We must embrace the foolishness of the Gospel and bear the reproach of Christ. Otherwise, we'll quickly become the kind of *lukewarm* Christian whom God spews out of His mouth. (See 1 Cor. 1:27; Heb. 11:26; Rev. 3:15-16.)

When contemplating our decision to lift high the Cross of Jesus Christ, we must not overlook this vital truth: Being set apart for Christ is not a hindrance to our Christian witness. Being set apart for Christ *is* our Christian witness.

If you are still unsure on this point, take some time to read Hebrews 11 and be reminded of what constitutes a true spiritual hero: not compliance with culture, but complete consecration to the King. Study the lives of the Christians throughout history who have most impacted the world for Christ. People like Vibia Perpetua, Athanasius, John Wycliffe, William Tyndale, John Knox, John Bunyan, Charles Spurgeon, Eric Liddell, C. T. Studd, Hudson Taylor, George Müller, Rees Howells, A. W. Tozer, William Booth, Amy Carmichael, Richard and Sabina Wurmbrand, Leonard Ravenhill, Paris Reidhead, Corrie ten Boom, George Whitefield, John Wesley, David Brainerd, E. M. Bounds, John Hyde, Jim and Elisabeth Elliot, D. L. Moody, Major W. Ian Thomas, Gladys Aylward, David Wilkerson, and Oswald Chambers.

Was it their ability to blend in with the world that caused them to influence others for eternity? Was it the fact that they kept up with cultural trends and knew how to gain approval and grow in popularity that helped them win souls? Just the opposite. What made these men and women unstoppable for God's kingdom was their willingness to be rejected, mocked, despised, and misunderstood. Many of them were scorned, falsely accused, and abused in extreme ways. But through it all, they remained more than conquerors, because they were living for something far greater than earthly applause.

Churches often assume that the world is rejecting Christianity today because we aren't enough like the culture. So they hire marketing companies to help the church become more culturally relevant. But the world isn't rejecting Christianity because we aren't enough like the culture. Rather, it's because we are *too much* like it. There is nothing different about our lives, nothing that proves we have found something bigger to live for than temporary pleasure, and certainly nothing that says we have found something worth dying for. We are pining after the same empty pursuits as non-believers are, enamored with the same celebrities, preoccupied with the same reality T.V. shows, and obsessed with the same pro sports teams. Why should they want what we have when our lives are no different from theirs, except for a few moral boundaries here and there?

It won't be flashy stage shows, coffee bars in our church lobbies, or slick marketing campaigns that will draw non-believers to our churches. And it won't be the example of lukewarm believers trying to be in touch with the culture and somehow make Christianity cool. Non-believers will only be drawn when they see something real, something powerful, something far beyond what pop culture could ever hope to offer.

Christ said, "And I, if I am lifted up from the earth, will draw all peoples to Myself" (Jn. 12:32). When Jesus Christ and His Cross are truly lifted up among us, our numbers will increase exponentially without us needing to imitate the world in order to get them there (see Acts 2:40-47).

When we stop being enamored by the world and start being captivated by our King, the world will stand back in wonder. Yes, non-believers may mock and revile us, but in the end they will be unable to deny the unshakable, unstoppable power of true Christianity, and they will be forever changed by what they see in our lives. Remember the powerful testimony of Stephen in the book of Acts? The unbelievers were so offended by his life and words that they stopped their ears and gnashed their teeth at him. But the Bible also says that "they were not able to resist the wisdom and the Spirit by which he spoke" (Acts 6:10).

Becoming a set-apart woman starts with a simple decision to leave the world and its passing pleasures and hold on to Christ and His Cross.

Are you ready to let go of lukewarm living and cling boldly to His Cross? The Cross may seem at first like the most undesirable place to be, yet the moment your hand grasps that splintery wood and you unashamedly declare, "I'm with Him!" it becomes the place of utmost joy and satisfaction.

SET-APARTNESS VERSUS LEGALISM

All of us have seen perversions of the concept of becoming separate from the world and being set apart for Christ. We are magnetically pulled toward anything that promises to make us "good" and "righteous" outside of Jesus Christ. Throughout history, people have tried to prove their own merit and earn spiritual brownie points by adhering to self-imposed rules. In today's world, examples of this are prevalent, from the Amish farmer who disavows all modern conveniences, to the Catholic nun who spends her life hidden away reciting rosaries in a convent, to the conservative Christian who won't associate with anyone who listens to music with a beat.

Many of us have experienced the damaging effects of professing Christians who have chosen to worship a set of rules, instead of wholeheartedly serving God. Maybe you grew up in a legalistic background, where music style and length of skirt mattered far more than purity of heart and mind. Maybe you have been hurt by Christians who divided the church over legalistic, peripheral issues.

Or maybe your stomach has been turned by seeing those who bear the name of Christ showcase their own personal convictions instead of pointing others to Him. I understand those feelings. Having traveled to and spoken at thousands of churches over the past twenty years, I've seen many well-meaning Christians ensnared and blinded by their own legalism, to the point where they have lost sight of the nature of

Christ. For example, at one Christian event a few years ago, a church leader informed me that I was unworthy to speak to a group of women about purity because I was wearing loose-fitting dress pants rather than a floor-length skirt. At another church event I was told I would not be allowed to get up and speak unless I took off my wedding ring, because "all jewelry is sinful."

Both legalism and worldliness are common in the Body of Christ today. Christians who are disturbed by the compromise prevalent in the modern church often try to solve the problem by relying on legalism and self-effort to keep them from the pitfalls of worldliness. Consequently, if today's churches aren't filled with carnal, compromising believers, they are often filled with prideful, self-righteous ones.

And because we have seen so many legalistic attempts to become separate from this world, many of us have a distorted view of what it means to be set apart for Christ. We worry it means that we'll become a stiff, somber, "holier-than-thou" type of woman who is far too concerned about following a set of rules to ever relax or enjoy life. But let me be clear: Legalism and true set-apartness are two very different things. Legalism *oppresses*, but true set-apartness *liberates*. Legalism *chokes* life, but true set-apartness *gives* life. Legalism is based upon *self-effort*, but true set-apartness is based upon the supernatural enabling *grace of God*. Legalism is based upon *rules*, but true set-apartness is based upon a *relationship* with the King of all kings.

In my book *Set-Apart Femininity* I told a true story about

two young women in China who were turned out of their homes and disowned by their families because of their faith in Christ.[3] They had no money, no protection, and nowhere to go, but they began walking from village to village, sharing the hope of the Gospel with everyone they encountered.

The girls knew that if they talked openly about their faith, their lives could be in danger. Yet they were so passionate about Jesus Christ that they couldn't help but speak of Him everywhere they went. As they talked about Him, their faces glowed. Even though they had nothing—not even a place to sleep—they were joyful and content. More than once, strangers came up to them and asked, "Why are your faces so shiny and radiant? What do you have that makes you so happy? Whatever it is, I need it in my life too!"

There was something so beautifully different about these two young women. They were set apart for Christ. They loved Him so deeply that they gladly and willingly put Him above all else, even though it had cost them everything and put their very lives at stake.

This is true set-apartness. It has nothing to do with adopting a set of rules in order to become more righteous. When you encounter Jesus Christ in a personal and life-changing way, He transforms you from the inside out. He gently cleanses away sin and worldliness from your soul, and causes you to love light and hate darkness. Your decision to come away with Christ and become consecrated to Him is an outflow of your overwhelming love and gratitude for Him. He has given everything for you. And in light of this glorious, astounding, unfathomable reality, the cry of your soul becomes, "Lord, may I give everything to You in return!" True set-apartness causes us to follow the example of Mary of Bethany, who willingly poured out her most precious possession upon the feet of Jesus. True set-apartness causes us to joyfully lay everything we have and everything we are at His feet without hesitation, simply because He is worthy (see Jn. 12:1-8).

When you are truly set apart for Christ, people don't look at your life and see a set of rules to follow. Rather, they look at your life and see *Jesus*—His life, His purity, His holiness, His joy, His selflessness, and His love. You are clinging to His Cross and His righteousness, and not to your own self-effort.

When you are truly set apart, you don't inwardly groan and complain about missing out on the pleasures of this world, or look for subtle ways to compromise. That's because you have discovered a far deeper, greater, infinitely more satisfying source of fulfillment than anything this world could ever offer. Your heart echoes the words of the psalmists when they declared, "In Your presence is fullness of joy; at Your right hand are pleasures forevermore" (Ps. 16:11) and "Better is one day in your courts than a thousand elsewhere" (Ps. 84:10, NIV).

When you are truly set apart, you don't need to rely on self-imposed rules in order to live a life that is consecrated to God. Rather, it becomes the greatest joy and delight of your heart to offer your life to Him and allow His Spirit to mold you into a pure and holy vessel, set apart for His purposes.

When you are truly set apart, you will lose your desire for worldly things and simply desire more of Him. As the old hymn so beautifully says, "The things of this earth will grow strangely dim in the light of His glory and grace."[4]

THE SECRET TO SET-APARTNESS

Have you ever read Scriptures such as Proverbs 31 (the qualities of a virtuous, godly woman) or 1 Corinthians 13 (the attributes of unconditional, Gospel love) and thought to yourself, *How could anyone ever really live that way?*

Many Christians have come to the conclusion that the epic visions of triumph and victory presented in Scripture are nothing more than poetic-sounding, larger-than-life ideals—sort of like those inspirational posters we see at the doctor's office or gym. We may be mentally motivated or emotionally moved by the beautiful promises and righteous standards presented in the Bible, but not many of us expect to live them out in everyday life—at least not on a consistent basis.

Several popular Christian books have been published in recent years with the purpose of assuring us that the lofty promises and standards of the Bible aren't truly achievable, so we should all stop feeling guilty about not personally attaining them. But God does not give us instructions that He won't enable us to carry out. If He said it, and He cannot lie, then what more is there to argue or discuss? Our God doesn't tease us by making promises to us that He doesn't intend to fulfill (see Num. 23:19).

So where does the discrepancy come in? Why is there such a big gap between the power of the Cross and the majesty of the Gospel as presented in Scripture, and the oft-mediocre reality of our daily lives?

The answer is simple: We have lost our understanding of the enabling power of God. The message of the Cross is much more than simply knowing and believing the Truth. It also means being supernaturally equipped by God's enabling grace to live a victorious life that would otherwise be impossible. When we try to rise up to God's standards without truly understanding the enabling power of God, we run smack into a brick wall of failure and disillusionment. But when we are transformed and equipped by God's enabling grace, we can confidently declare along with Paul, "I can do all things through Christ who strengthens me" (Phil. 4:13).

Whether God is calling you to come away from sin and worldliness or from legalism and self-righteousness, the solution is the same: "Jesus Christ and Him crucified" (1 Cor. 2:2). Corrie ten Boom articulated this well with her statement, "When I try, I fail. When I trust, He succeeds."

Coming to the Cross means much more than believing that Christ died for your sins. It means exchanging all that you are for all that He is. It means being overtaken by His divine indwelling power, which supernaturally equips you to live a holy, triumphant life that would be impossible on your own. When you grasp the mystery of "Christ in you, the hope of glory" (Col. 1:27), you will grasp the secret to true set-apartness.

When the life and Spirit of Christ dwells within you, you have the power to be holy as He is holy (see 1 Pet. 1:15-16). You no longer need to be enslaved to sin or helpless against the temptations of the world. You are set apart for Him, not because of your own righteousness, but because you are clothed in His.

I like what Evan Hopkins says about this truth: "Think what it is we really possess, if Christ is in us. . . . All power, all grace, all purity, and all fulness, absolutely everything to make all grace abound towards us, in us, and through us, are stored up in Him who verily dwells within us."[5]

Many believers have resigned themselves to the attitude, "I'll always struggle with sin; I shouldn't expect victory this side of heaven." We read Paul's statement in Romans 7:24— "O wretched man that I am! Who will deliver me from this body of death?"—and reason, "Well, if Paul couldn't overcome sin, who am I to think I'm any different?" But the answer to Paul's question is presented clearly in the next sentence: "Thanks be to *God* through *Jesus Christ our Lord*!" (Ro. 7:25, ESV, emphasis added). Because of the work of the Cross and the enabling grace of Christ that dwells within us, we have the power to "reckon [ourselves] to be dead indeed to sin, but alive to God in Christ Jesus our Lord" (Ro. 6:11). Our "old man" has been crucified with Christ (see Ro. 6:6). Therefore, we are free to no longer serve sin, but to "walk in the light as He is in the light" (1 Jn. 1:7).

If you hear the voice of God's Spirit calling you toward greater levels of purity and consecration unto Him, beware of hiding behind the excuse, "I'll always be weak and sinful; I can't expect anything more." Such logic will be deadly to your soul and toxic to your spiritual life.

Consider the following words of wisdom: Andrew Bonar wrote, "It is more humbling for us to *take what grace offers*, than to bewail our wants and worthlessness."[6] And the pastor Adoniram Judson Gordon said, "How many true Christians toil on, bearing burdens and assuming responsibilities far too great for their natural strength, utterly forgetful that the mighty Burden-Bearer of the world is with them to do for them and through them that which they have undertaken to accomplish alone."[7]

Embracing the enabling grace of God to overcome sinful strongholds does not mean living in "sinless perfection" and never stumbling again (see Phil. 3:12). But neither should we expect to be controlled by the bondage of sin or legalism. Let us no longer underestimate the power of the Cross or doubt God's willingness and ability to transform us into "new creations" in Christ (see 2 Cor. 5:17)! (For more on this subject, I encourage you to listen to the messages "Overcoming Sin" and "The Manifold Wonder of Grace," available for free download at our website, www.ellerslie.com.)

THE POWER OF THE CROSS

Jackie Pullinger, a longtime missionary to China, wrote about sharing the Gospel with a woman who had been a prostitute for more than forty years. This woman had been rejected, abused, and mistreated in nearly every way imaginable. Yet neither coddling, sympathy, or psychological principles delivered this woman from despair and changed her from the inside out—the undiluted message of the Cross did. She was changed by the transforming power of Jesus Christ and Him crucified. She became a new creature in Christ, and, as Jackie described it, "she had all her life again."[8]

It's easy to believe that because of specific things we have been through, the Gospel can't truly be applied to our lives in all its fullness and power. We assume that if we've been through extreme difficulty or disappointment, we are entitled to a "special version" of Truth, perhaps seasoned with a few sympathetic words such as, "Don't worry, God knows your situation is unique. You can't be expected to apply biblical Truth to your life the way others do!"

When we play this "special circumstances" card, we are creating a makeshift excuse to not take Jesus Christ at His Word. There is no situation that the power of the Cross cannot permeate and transform, and there is no wound that His cleansing blood cannot heal. In fact, the more extreme the circumstances, the more opportunity for His supernatural grace to be demonstrated in all its life-changing power.

Throughout Christian history, the Gospel has spread like wildfire whenever the most destitute and notorious people have been radically changed by its power. In all the great revivals, people were drawn to the Gospel when they saw alcoholics forsake their addictions and prostitutes begin to live in purity.

If the message of the Cross can offer such freedom and triumph for people like these, can it not do the same for us?

Personally, I have felt the most impact of God's Truth in my life not when things have been easy but when things have been the most difficult. Eric and I have been through tremendous trials and struggles over the years. Anyone who has been in Christian ministry for twenty years, as we have, knows that it's like living on a battlefield. We have taken many bullets along the way, both from the Enemy's spiritual attacks and from people who have reviled and rejected us. We have experienced intense personal grief, such as losing our second child to a miscarriage, and we have been stabbed in the back by friends we deeply trusted. We have faced extreme financial crisis through the dishonesty and corruption of others. We have been threatened, cursed, and called terrible names publicly. Most of the details of these experiences can't be shared without dishonoring certain people, so we don't often write or speak about them.

It is not because we haven't been through trials that we speak so confidently about the transforming power of the Gospel, but because we have faced so many. We have experienced the victory that comes when we cling to the Cross and allow His divine power to give us strength far beyond any strength we could ever find within ourselves. That doesn't mean that every day is filled with sunshine and roses. There are times when we must wrestle through the tears, the hurt, the confusion, and the fear until we finally "break through" to a clear, Truth-filled perspective. But when we wrestle for it, it always comes.

As a friend of Amy Carmichael's pointed out, "Faith has

nothing to do with circumstances. It deals entirely with the Word of God."⁹ As you are contemplating the set-apart, victorious, triumphant Christian life that God has called you to, beware of an attitude that says, "But my situation is different. I can't experience that kind of joy and freedom because . . ."

Even if you don't sense an immediate victory in the midst of your difficult circumstances, that doesn't mean God doesn't intend to give it to you. Continue to pursue His promises until they have become reality in your daily life. And soon you will be able to confidently declare along with Paul, "Thanks be to God who *always* leads us in triumph in Christ" (2 Cor. 2:14, emphasis added).

The Cross of Jesus Christ, as the old hymn says, is an "emblem of suffering and shame."¹⁰ But it is also the place of the most glorious redemption in history. Because of the Cross, we have passed from despair to hope, from defeat to victory, and from death to everlasting life. To become the set-apart women He has called us to be, we cannot merely take the benefits of the Cross; we must also be willing to bear its reproach.

True life comes not when we stand *near* to Jesus Christ and Him crucified, but when we cling unashamedly to His Cross and lift it high for all the world to see.

Are you ready to take hold of that splintery wood?

LET'S TALK ABOUT IT

🗨 *Group Study and Discussion*

1. READ HEBREWS 11:24-26. What does it mean to choose the reproach of Christ over the passing pleasures of sin? Why do we so often shy away from bearing His reproach?

2. READ ROMANS 1:16 AND 1 CORINTHIANS 2:2. What is the difference between standing near the Cross and clinging to it? When we cling to the Cross and lift it high for all the world to see, how will our lives impact non-believers? How is this different from using worldly methods to draw people to Christianity?

TAKE IT DEEPER

📖 *Personal Study and Reflection*

READ: REVELATION 3:15-16

REFLECT: Am I waffling between worldliness and Christianity? Am I willing to cling unashamedly to His Cross, even if it means I must bear His reproach? In what areas of my life do I feel Him calling me to embrace wholehearted devotion to Him?

READ: JOHN 15:19

REFLECT: Am I willing to become separate from this world in order to be consecrated to Christ? What changes do I feel He is asking me to make in order to do so?

READ: COLOSSIANS 1:27

REFLECT: Am I ready to yield to the enabling power of God to live the kind of set-apart life I could never attain on my own? In what areas of my life do I specifically need His enabling grace to equip me to live as I ought? (Take some time to invite His enabling grace to equip you in these areas.)

CHAPTER THREE

Awake, My Soul

Exchanging Apathy for Passion

Never be lacking in zeal, but keep your spiritual fervor, serving the Lord.

ROMANS 12:11, NIV

Be on the alert with all perseverance and petition.

EPHESIANS 6:18, NASB

Is prayer your steering wheel or your spare tire?

CORRIE TEN BOOM

We are too busy to pray, and so we are too busy to have power. We have a great deal of activity but we accomplish little; many services but few conversions; much machinery but few results.

R. A. TORREY, *How to Obtain Fulness of Power in Christian Life and Service*

A MOM OF SIX ONCE TOLD ME, "I'm too busy *not* to pray!"

Therein lies the secret to a thriving relationship with Jesus Christ. But many of us might admit that we've got our thinking regarding busyness and prayer backward. Let's be honest—for us as busy women, prayer often becomes that one project we'll "get to eventually," like cleaning the cobwebs from the vaulted ceiling or writing a cookbook. With so many demands on our time and energy, most of us conclude that the only real prayer life we can have are those short bursts of heavenly appeal ("Help, Lord!") during the stressful moments of our day.

In the real world, prayer just doesn't always seem practical. I mean, how can we possibly make our relationship with Christ the highest priority of our lives when we are mothering little ones, or obligated to friends and relatives, or cultivating a relationship, or working long hours in our job, or managing a heavy class load, or planning a wedding, or carrying the weight of full-time ministry?

I've struggled with this dilemma many times. There have been many seasons when I have attempted to "coast" spiritually, to put my prayer life on hold while I rush around in a frenzy, trying to get everything done. Like the time a few years ago when our four children were all ages four and under. Three were in diapers, two were in high chairs, and the noise level in our house rivaled the Whos down in Whoville on Christmas morning. Spending quality time with Christ each day felt next to impossible.

I reasoned, *Surely God understands how hard I've been working, how tired I am, and how impractical it is to fit prayer and Bible study into my life right now. He won't mind if I just say a few hurried statements to Him here and there, whenever I can fit it in!*

But I have learned that this reasoning quickly leads to spiritual apathy. My excuses hinder my relationship with Christ, and I begin to wane in my commitment to pursue Him with all my heart, soul, mind, and strength. I start replacing spiritual passion with busyness, and my prayer life grows lax.

It's not that spending a certain amount of time in prayer each day somehow makes me more righteous. But time in God's presence is what gives me the spiritual fuel I need to live the victorious Christian life He has called me to. Time alone with God stokes my spiritual fire; it keeps my love for Him strong and thriving.

We don't have much difficulty understanding this principle when it comes to cultivating earthly relationships. We know that to maintain intimacy with our spouse, we must spend purposeful time together on a regular basis. We recognize that our friendships can't flourish if we don't invest ourselves into those people often. We see the importance of spending quality time with our children. But when it comes to our relationship with God, we are often full of excuses: "Oh, He'll understand. He knows it's just not practical right now. I'll get to prayer later."

A. W. Tozer wrote, "The man [or woman] who would

know God must give time to Him."[1] What a simple and profound truth, but one that is all too easy to forget amid the busyness of our daily lives.

Not long ago I spoke to a group of Christian women about the importance of keeping prayer and time with God a high priority, even if it means that we must get less sleep or skip certain social and leisure activities to do so. Many responded enthusiastically to this reminder, but some balked. One woman remarked, "Sometimes we just need to let go of these 'unrealistic spiritual expectations' and take a nap!"

Many Christians today have this attitude. Anytime someone starts talking about having tireless spiritual passion and pursuing Christ with all our heart, soul, mind, and strength, we are tempted to reason, *Oh, that's completely unrealistic. No one can be that passionate about Christ at all times. If we try, we'll only end up putting unhealthy pressure upon ourselves and getting exhausted. It can't be done.*

But Jesus says otherwise. He tells us, "Blessed are those servants whom the master, when he comes, will find watching" (Lk. 12:37). The word *watching* in this context literally means "to be roused from sleep, to be awake, to be on the alert."

In a culture that promotes busyness and self-indulgence, many of us have adopted a lackadaisical mind-set toward our relationship with Christ. Few of us possess any lasting spiritual passion. And we don't pursue it, because we don't think it is possible to find it.

In Romans 12:11 Paul said, "Never be lacking in zeal, but keep your spiritual fervor, serving the Lord" (NIV). I have often read that verse and wondered, *How is it possible to* never *lose my zeal for God and to* always *keep my spiritual fervor?* Certainly it is possible, or God would not have put it in the Bible.

When I think of set-apart Christian women who have lived out this command, I remember the lives of many heroic women (some of whom I referred to earlier) whose example of relentless, unwavering spiritual passion never ceases to amaze and inspire me. I remember Amy Carmichael, who went to the mission field as a young woman and rescued over a thousand children in India amid intense persecution, danger, financial distress, and ill health. I remember Gladys Aylward, who risked her life again and again to bring the Gospel to China during a war—even to the point where her clothes were riddled with bullet holes and her picture was on wanted posters. I remember Esther Ahn Kim, who maintained a passionate relationship with Christ even during years of torture and imprisonment. And I remember scores of other valiant women such as Mary Slessor, Elizabeth Fry, Catherine Booth, and Corrie ten Boom, whose spiritual flames burned brightly amid staggering obstacles and trials.

When I study the lives of these women who pursued Jesus Christ amid some of the greatest difficulties and trials imaginable, I realize I have no excuse for spiritual slothfulness.

Most of us desire to know God more than we do. We sense our need for more of His presence and power in our daily lives. We feel an aching spiritual hunger in our souls for something more in our relationship with Him. And yet we often balk at doing the one thing that would bring us closer to Him: spending time in His presence.

The Bible offers a practical solution for growing closer to God: "Draw near to God and He will draw near to you" (Jas. 4:8). Are we willing to do whatever it takes to draw near to Jesus? Are we willing to lose sleep, food, productivity, social status, and "downtime" in order to make time with God the highest priority of our lives? Do we have a spiritual determination that says, "No obstacle will keep me from my King—even if I must go up to the rooftop and break through the house tiles to get to Him, just as the lame man's friends did in order to get to Jesus" (see Mk. 2:4)? Or do we make halfhearted attempts to spend time in prayer, and when distractions arise say, "Oh well, at least I tried."

Whenever I catch myself saying, "I have too much to get done today to spend time in prayer," I know that spiritual apathy has crept in, and that I've allowed the cares of this world to keep me from my God.

Jesus told a poignant parable to His disciples about making excuses that is perhaps one of the most convicting stories in the Bible.

A certain man gave a great supper and invited many,
and sent his servant at supper time to say to those
who were invited, "Come, for all things are now
ready." But they all with one accord began to make
excuses. The first said to him, "I have bought a piece
of ground, and I must go and see it. I ask you to

have me excused." And another said, "I have bought five yoke of oxen, and I am going to test them. I ask you to have me excused." Still another said, "I have married a wife, and therefore I cannot come." (Lk. 14:16-20)

Our loving Redeemer waits at the banquet table. He has prepared a beautiful feast for us; He desires to fill us with His very life and satisfy the deepest needs within our souls. He does not invite us to His banquet demandingly, but *longingly*. He shed His blood so that He could be in relationship with us. And He stands at the table, eagerly waiting to commune with us. We have the amazing, astounding, thrilling privilege of being invited daily into the presence of the King of all kings, to come before His throne of grace and to partake of all that He is. Yet how often do we reply, *I cannot come; I have something more important to do. I ask you to have me excused!*

Oh, what a heartbreaking response! It's as if someone is offering us a handful of diamonds, and we choose a pile of pebbles instead.

I often think of Mary and Martha when I'm struggling to keep my spiritual priorities in check. It seemed impractical for Martha to stop bustling around the kitchen and sit at Jesus' feet, as Mary was doing. She must have been thinking, *Surely Jesus understands how much work I need to get done, and how many responsibilities I have on my plate right now! Surely He knows I can't just drop everything to spend time with Him!*

And yet, Jesus told Martha, "You are worried and troubled about many things. But one thing is needed" (Lk. 10:41-42). What was that "one thing" that Martha needed? To sit at Jesus' feet and receive His Word. That was the only way she would ever find the strength and grace to do everything else she was called to do.

Martha's serving and hospitality were not the problem. The problem was that she was attempting to do these things in her own ability, without making time with Jesus her highest priority. As a result Martha was worried and "distracted with much serving" (Lk. 10:40). What a perfect description of so many busy women today! When we serve our families or work hard at our tasks without the undergirding strength that comes through time with God, it quickly leads to burnout and stress, just as it did for Martha. And the more burned out and stressed we become, the more we try to convince ourselves that we are too exhausted and frenzied to fit prayer into our lives.

It is only when we choose to live by the "too busy *not* to pray" principle that we will experience a thriving walk with Christ and, thus, a life that really works.

MAKING THE EXCHANGE

We can't muster up genuine spiritual fervor. It only comes through consistent prayer, meditation on Truth, heartfelt worship, and intimate communion with the King of all kings.

But how do we put prayer and time with God in their

rightful place when every spare moment of our time is already accounted for?

A set-apart woman is committed to cultivating a passionate daily relationship with Christ, despite the obstacles that may stand in her way. I would like to share some of the practical steps that have most helped me overcome the roadblocks and excuses that hinder me from making prayer a priority each day. I hope they will help you do the same.

1. DON'T CONSULT YOUR *Emotions*

Corrie ten Boom once said, "Don't pray when you feel like it. Have an appointment with the Lord and keep it." I have found this principle to be extremely helpful in making prayer my highest priority. Often, prayer is not what I "feel" like doing. But when I set a regular appointment with God and honor it, no matter what my body or emotions might say, my soul greatly benefits.

If we make a habit of doing whatever we "feel like" rather than what God's Spirit is asking of us, we can be sure that our relationship with Jesus Christ will suffer. Instead of pursuing Christ with true devotion, we halfheartedly read our Bible for five minutes, then click on our computer because it feels more exciting to check our e-mail than to labor through the Scriptures. Instead of making personal sacrifices to set aside time for prayer, we give in to laziness and then come up with elaborate justifications as to why we are too busy to fit it in.

Daily life is filled with hundreds of choices to either give in to our selfish whims or yield to Christ's Spirit and obey

His commands. For example, when the alarm goes off in the morning, do you yield to the beckoning whisper of Christ's Spirit, asking you to get up and spend time with Him, or do you listen to your own desire to stay in bed and push the snooze button over and over again until it's too late to have a quiet time?

Loving our King is first an act of the will, a choice to put Him first, no matter what our feelings may say.

One of my greatest inspirations is a woman named Elizabeth Fry, a Quaker who lived several centuries ago. Though she had a husband, numerous children, and a full life, every morning upon rising she began asking the question, "Lord, how can I bring You glory today?" Soon, God led her to a women's prison in her community, where the inmates were being treated like animals. She began to visit the prison, bringing food, care, comfort, love, and hope to women who had lost their desire to live. Elizabeth became a powerful tool in the hand of God to deliver the Gospel to the poor and discarded. Women's lives were changed, and new legislation for prison standards was adopted. And soon, God used Elizabeth to transform the entire prison system in all of Europe. She became one of the most influential Christian women who has ever lived, all from beginning each morning with the question, "Lord, how can I bring You glory today?"

When we choose to consult the Spirit of Truth instead of our own feelings, we make different decisions in our daily lives, decisions that place God's priorities above our own wants. If you have been letting your feelings trump your commitment to spending time with Christ, choose a different attitude when you first wake up in the morning. Instead of consulting your emotions with questions such as, "What do I want to get out of today?" or "How can I avoid the discomfort of getting out of bed right now?" adopt a new mind-set: "Lord, this is Your day. Show me how to use each moment for Your glory."

Remember, you may not have a "mountaintop experience" each time you pray and seek God. But as you learn to love Him as an act of your will (following His pattern whether you feel like it or not), your emotions and feelings will eventually follow suit. Soon, it will become your greatest delight to give your life to Him, and you will be able to echo the words of the psalmist who said, "I delight to do Your will, O my God" (Ps. 40:8).

2. BE WILLING TO MAKE *Sacrifices*

In my current stage of life, I've found that the best time for me to pray and be with God is early in the morning, before my children wake up. Getting up early is not easy for me, especially when I've been awakened by kids several times in the middle of the night! But, as Elisabeth Elliot wrote,

> The best time for most people is early morning—
> not because most of us love jumping out of bed,
> but because it is the only time of day when we can
> be fairly sure of not being interrupted and because it
> is best to commune with God before you commune

with people. Your attitude toward them will then arise out of your life in Him. Offering to God the first hour of the day is a token of consecration of all of our time.[2]

Scripture puts a high value on waking up early, even before dawn, and giving the firstfruits of our day to God through praying, worshiping, and seeking His face:

> You are my God; early will I seek You; my soul thirsts for You.
> (PS. 63:1)

> Awake, my glory! Awake, lute and harp! I will awaken the dawn.
> (PS. 57:8)

> [The virtuous woman] also rises while it is yet night.
> (PROV. 31:15)

Jesus Himself set for us a clear example of rising early to seek the Father's face: "Now in the morning, having risen a long while before daylight, He went out and departed to a solitary place; and there He prayed" (Mk. 1:35).

There is something so right about rising early to seek God in prayer. It is the ultimate way to deny self (see Mt. 16:24)— to silence our excuses and yield to the Spirit of God. It's an opportunity to declare with our lives, not just our lips, that

Jesus truly is our most important priority. It gives the Spirit of God the first say over our time and priorities.

John Bunyan wrote, "He who runs from God in the morning will scarcely find Him the rest of the day." I have found this to be true in my own life. Whenever I allow myself to oversleep and miss my time in God's presence, the entire day feels "off." But when I discipline myself and make early-morning prayer a nonnegotiable, I walk in the sweet presence of my King for the rest of my day. Jesus said, "Seek first the kingdom of God" (Mt. 6:33). When I apply this command to my prayer life and make seeking Him my first act of the day, every other area of my life comes into alignment.

Whenever possible, I get up early to consecrate the first-fruits of my day to God by spending time in His Word and in prayer. In those seasons when it has not been possible for me to get up before my children (for instance, when I have been up all night for multiple weeks with a newborn, or struggling with a physical issue that impacted my sleep) I have had to come up with creative solutions to make time for prayer. Sometimes, I've had a helper come to the house first thing in the morning to take over with the kids while I get a shower and have a quiet time. Other times, Eric has stepped in to manage the morning routine and supervise the kids so that I can get that much-needed time in prayer and in the Word. Once my kids got past the infant/toddler stage, I found that having a regular time each morning for them to sit and quietly read books or watch an edifying video provided an opportunity for me to spend time alone with God.

If it is truly not possible for you to build prayer into your early mornings, then designate another time during the day when you can be relatively sure you won't be interrupted. The key to a disciplined prayer life is regularity, consistency, and commitment!

Evenings are another great time to build in periods for regular prayer, though it's not often what most of us are in the mood for at the end of a long day. When I get my kids into bed and the house is finally calm, I typically feel like unwinding with a good book or browsing the Internet to find ideas and inspiration for various household projects. But I've learned that right after getting the kids settled for the night is a wonderful time for Eric and me to pray together. We're able to pray about important needs in our family or ministry. This not only builds deeper unity and spiritual like-mindedness between the two of us, but also strengthens our individual relationships with Christ and makes Him the priority of our evenings. It's not that we never spend time at night reading, talking, or browsing online, but whenever we make prayer our most important nighttime activity, both our marriage and our spiritual lives are greatly blessed.

John "Praying" Hyde said, "Early in the morning, 4 or 5 o'clock . . . and late at night to 12 or 1 o'clock. In college or at parties at home, I used to keep such hours for myself or pleasure, and can I not do as much for God and souls?"[3] What convicting words! Are we are willing to make daily personal sacrifices in order to put our relationship with Christ first?

3. GATHER THE RIGHT *Tools*

A lot of women ask me how to structure their prayer times. It's one thing to set aside specific time to pray, but then what? How do we connect with the King of the universe in a significant way? There is no magic formula for prayer and seeking God, and every prayer time will probably be a little different. But a good rule of thumb is this: Make it all about Him, instead of all about you. Meditate on His goodness, faithfulness, and majesty. Praise Him for all He has done in your life. Thank Him for His astounding work of redemption in your soul. Dwell upon His amazing promises and reckon them as fact, no matter what your feelings or past experience might say. Worship songs, Scripture, and Christ-centered books or sermons can all assist you in doing this. (See the Recommended Resources at the back of the book for some of my favorites.)

Of course it's not wrong to tell God about your fears, hopes, dreams, and feelings. In fact, the Bible tells us to cast our cares upon Him (see 1 Pet. 5:7) and to present our requests to God (see Phil. 4:6). But far too many of us spend the majority of our prayer and quiet times meditating upon how we feel rather than upon who God is. When we behold the beauty of our King, our own thoughts, feelings, and worries fade into the background. As we delight in Him, He grants us the desires of our hearts. As we turn our eyes to Him and away from ourselves, He "fills all in all" (Eph. 1:23).

I love to keep a prayer journal because it allows me to

record the faithfulness of God in my life. Whenever I am walking through a season where my faith is being tested, it is uplifting to read back over my journal throughout the past years or months, and see how many times God has come through for me.

Spend some time thinking through what tools could assist you in having more effective prayer and quiet times. Can you set aside an area of the house that is quiet and free from distractions? Can you download some worship music or audio Scripture to listen to while you pray and meditate upon Him? *The Word of Promise* is one of my favorite audio Bibles, because it is professionally dramatized and enhanced with beautiful music. Starting out a prayer time by playing a few of the psalms from *The Word of Promise* has proven a wonderful tool to help usher me into the presence of God.

Ask God to show you the practical things you can do not only to guard your daily appointment with Him, but also to make that time as powerful and Christ-centered as possible.

4. EMBRACE GODLY *Discipline*

The apostle Paul said, "I discipline my body and bring it into subjection, lest, when I have preached to others, I myself should become disqualified" (1 Cor. 9:27).

The word *discipline* has almost become taboo in today's modern Christian world. It conjures up images of legalism and lists of rules and regulations. Yet godly discipline is nothing of the sort. It is an act of worship—crucifying our selfish agenda in order to surrender to Christ's pure and perfect agenda (see Ro. 12:1). Discipline does not bring misery and restriction into our lives. Rather, it brings glorious freedom. When our bodies and emotions are subject to the Spirit of God, we are free to live as He calls us to live rather than being enslaved to our selfish desires. We are able to give our time, our energy, and our lives fully to the things of His kingdom.

During the seasons of my life in which I have embraced a disciplined lifestyle as an act of worship, my intimacy with Christ has flourished. But whenever I say, "It doesn't matter how much time I spend in prayer," I find that my relationship with Him slips to the back burner, and I end up talking a lot *about* Him without really *knowing* Him. It is not the mere act of "being disciplined" that draws me close to Christ. But discipline allows me to hear His voice, understand His Truth, and connect with His heart in a way that is impossible when I'm controlled by selfishness and apathy.

It is important to recognize that godly discipline and human willpower are two different things. Willpower only lasts temporarily and is dependent upon our own ability. Godly discipline goes far beyond mere human "oomph" and comes through yielding to His Spirit and relying on His grace. It is impossible in our own strength. There have been many early mornings when I have whispered, "Lord, I do not have the energy to get out of bed. Please infuse me with Your strength. Give me the grace to do what You have called me to do!" Whenever I pray this prayer, I find that He enables me by His grace to do what would otherwise be impossible in my own strength.

Even if personal discipline doesn't come naturally for you, remember that anyone can embrace godly discipline. All you must do is take steps of obedience and call upon Him for the strength and grace to do what you could never do on your own.

Here are some practical ways to start building godly discipline into your life:

- *Memorize a simple Scripture to recite the moment your alarm goes off.* I love to whisper Psalm 118:24 first thing in the morning: "This is the day the LORD has made; we will rejoice and be glad in it." Meditating upon Truth turns my focus toward my King and helps me to ignore my body's plea to pull the covers back over my head.

- *Recruit an accountability partner with whom you can honestly share the areas in your life that need greater discipline.* Ask that person to pray with you and encourage you as you seek to make changes in these areas, by the grace of God. Having a trusted friend with whom you can share your failures and successes can make a tremendous difference in pushing you toward a more disciplined lifestyle, enabled by God's grace.

- *Start gradually.* If you are used to waking up at 9 a.m. and you try to switch cold turkey to a 5 a.m. wake-up time, chances are you will wane in your commitment after a day or two. Instead, try setting your alarm for twenty minutes earlier for the first couple of days. Then, set it for another twenty minutes earlier and work on that new discipline for a few days.

Continue this pattern until you have reached the wake-up time that you feel God is asking of you. Let your body get used to change over a period of a few weeks. You can do the same for lengthening your prayer sessions. If you have only been spending five minutes a day in prayer, don't jump to an hour (unless of course you believe that God is asking you to do so!). Instead, add an additional five minutes each day until you reach the length that you feel God desires.

Remember that practical steps such as these should never become a "formula for holiness" or "means of righteousness" in themselves. Godly discipline is an act of surrender. It is a practical way that we can learn to deny ourselves and take up our cross to follow Christ (see Mt. 16:24). Every step to build godly discipline into our lives should be an outflow of our love for Christ, not a way to gain spiritual brownie points or prove our own righteousness (since we have none outside of Christ anyway!).

5. GET BACK UP *on the Horse*

Most of us will go through unusual seasons in which regular, consistent prayer just doesn't happen. It may be the birth of a child, a difficult pregnancy, a hospital stay, a family emergency, and so on, when every spare moment of our time and energy is given to "survival mode." Recently Eric and I walked through a season like this. For several weeks, we were in the midst of an intense crisis involving several people that we were close to. And while we did pray during that season, it was just short bursts of crying out to God whenever we could steal away for a few minutes.

I knew that God was giving us grace for what we were walking through and that He was sustaining us super-naturally, even though it wasn't possible for us to spend hours in prayer each day. But as soon as things calmed down and life returned to a relatively normal pace, I knew it was time to build regular, consistent prayer back into our lives.

When life seems to buck me off my normal prayer routine, I have learned to rise up on the strength of God and get back in the saddle as soon as I possibly can. Instead of feeling like I somehow have to play spiritual catch-up when I haven't spent much time in prayer for a while, I rest in the comforting fact that I can pick up right where I left off. No matter what I have walked through, my God is unchanging, and He is always ready and waiting for me to cast my cares upon Him!

6. CHOOSE THE IMPORTANT *over the Urgent*

Several years ago, Eric and I felt God calling us into a season of intensive prayer. There were a handful of areas in our lives and ministry that we sensed God wanted us to wrestle for spiritually until we saw a clear breakthrough. For us, this meant spending several hours in prayer each day for a period of several months. There was nothing practical about this commitment. We had young children at home, a church and ministry to lead, and book deadlines to meet. Most days, my task list felt overwhelming. I couldn't imagine spending less time in "work mode" and more time in "prayer mode." How would anything ever get done? Wouldn't I just fall further and further behind and become even more stressed than I already was? I thought of Jesus' promise: "Seek first the kingdom of God . . . and all these things shall be added to you" (Mt. 6:33). Eric and I decided to put those words to the test.

We began to make room for prayer even when we didn't feel like it was realistic. Instead of being driven by our task list, we became driven by our desire to spend time in God's presence. It's not that we neglected our responsibilities. Rather, we *realigned our priorities* around prayer. And it was truly astounding to see what God did in our lives as a result.

Tasks that normally would have taken four hours now took one. Projects that we assumed would take weeks were done in days. Our productivity multiplied exponentially, even though we were spending less time on our tasks and more time in prayer. We were witnessing firsthand the principle of "seeking His kingdom first." God has promised that when we build our lives around His priorities, He will make sure all our needs are taken care of. But most of us are not willing to allow this principle to be proven true in our lives.

On two different occasions, the disciples fished all night long and caught nothing. But when Jesus came and stood in their midst, they let down their net once and caught such an abundance that they didn't even have room in their boat to contain it all (see Lk. 5:4 and Jn. 21:3-6).

When prayer is missing from our lives and we are controlled by the tyranny of the urgent, we spend countless time and energy trying to make our lives work, constantly failing and beating our head against the wall in frustration. But as it says in Psalm 1, when we meditate upon our Lord day and night, we become like a tree that "brings forth . . . fruit"— and everything we do just somehow works. Life becomes fruitful instead of frustrating.

Next time you are tempted to choose busyness over prayer, remember the secret to making life work: *putting Jesus first*. (To go deeper into this subject, I recommend the book *Tyranny of the Urgent!* by Charles Hummel.)

7. TUNE OUT THE *Enemy's Voice*

Whenever I have walked through a season of spiritual apathy, my attempts to return to a Christ-centered focus are usually met with a lot of resistance from the Enemy. No sooner do I sit down to have a prayer time than the Enemy whispers mockingly: "Your prayers aren't going to make a difference. You may as well not even try!" Or, "You are putting unhealthy expectations on yourself. You can always pray later. Right now you need to put your spiritual life on hold and take care of *you*." Or, "Look how many times you've made mistakes this week. God is far too unhappy with you to listen to your prayers!"

If I entertain any of these suggestions, my prayer time quickly goes down the drain. We must recognize the Enemy's lies for what they are—lies—and kick those thoughts out the moment they attempt to enter the door of our minds. No matter how convincing the lie may seem, any thought or notion that pulls us away from Jesus Christ is not coming from God. The Bible says that we are to take "every thought captive to the obedience of Christ" (2 Cor. 10:5, NASB).

One of the most effective ways that I have found to take "enemy thoughts" captive is to answer back with Truth, just as Jesus did when the Enemy tempted Him in the wilderness (see Mt. 4:1-11). Memorizing and meditating upon Scripture helps me fire Truth back at the Enemy whenever he attempts to bombard me with lies. Lies cannot remain when we stand on God's Truth!

The book of Nehemiah provides an amazing picture of resisting the Enemy's lies. As Nehemiah was rebuilding the wall around Jerusalem, his enemies mocked him, distracted him, and threatened him. They sent false prophets to warn him that he must flee into the temple to hide. They accused him of rebelling against the king. They made plans to slay him and his workers during the night (see Neh. 4:11-12). Yet each time, Nehemiah met their lies with Truth, and continued in what God had called him to do. As a result, the enemies' plot came to nothing, and Nehemiah succeeded in the work that God had called him to do.

Don't be surprised if the Enemy attacks you when you take steps forward to pursue Jesus Christ. Leonard Ravenhill said, "Men of prayer must be men of steel, for they will be assaulted by Satan even before they attempt to assault his kingdom."[4] This principle also applies to us as women!

Be on guard and ready to fight Satan's lies with God's Truth. As you make a habit of tuning out the Enemy's "noise" and doing what you know God has called you to do, you will be successful in your spiritual pursuits, just as Nehemiah was successful in building the wall. (For more on this subject, I recommend the message "The 9 Lies," available for free download at www.ellerslie.com.)

Most of us would say that our highest priority is Jesus Christ. But does our lifestyle prove this statement true? It is all too easy to put Him first theoretically instead of practically. In order to exchange apathy for passion and become set apart for Christ, we must honor Him with our actions and our daily decisions, not just our words (see Mt. 15:8).

There is no better cure for spiritual apathy than to make Him the highest priority of your day. As you take practical steps of obedience to draw near to Him, He will draw near to you and ignite spiritual passion in your soul. As you tune out the cares of this life and spend time in His presence, your lukewarm faith will soon be replaced with a holy spiritual fire. Remember, if we seek Him diligently, the Bible promises that He *will* be found! (See Jer. 29:13.)

LET'S TALK ABOUT IT

Group Study and Discussion

1. **READ ROMANS 12:11.** What causes us to lose our spiritual passion? How can it be regained?

2. **READ PSALM 57:8.** What is the difference between going through the motions of Christianity and serving Him with fervor? Why is it important to make prayer and personal time with Christ a priority, even when it doesn't seem convenient?

TAKE IT DEEPER

Personal Study and Reflection

READ: 1 CORINTHIANS 9:27

REFLECT: Am I willing to embrace godly discipline in order to make my prayer life a priority? What practical areas of my life will need to change in order for me to do so?

READ: PROVERBS 28:26

REFLECT: When it comes to cultivating my prayer life, am I consulting my feelings and whims instead of obeying the Spirit of God? Am I willing to make prayer a priority even when I don't "feel" like praying? If yes, what specific changes will that mean for my daily lifestyle?

READ: MATTHEW 6:33

REFLECT: Am I seeking the kingdom of God first, or has my relationship with Christ been moved to the back burner? Do I believe that when I put Him first, every other area of my life will be blessed as well? How can I begin to live according to this reality?

CHAPTER FOUR

Redeeming the Time

Exchanging Temporal Distractions for True Satisfaction

See then that you walk circumspectly, not as fools but as wise, redeeming the time, because the days are evil.

EPHESIANS 5:15-16

She . . . does not eat the bread of idleness.

PROVERBS 31:27

Live every day as if the Son of Man were at the door, and gear your thinking to the fleeting moment. Just how can it be redeemed? Walk as if the next step would carry you across the threshold of Heaven.

JIM ELLIOT, *Shadow of the Almighty*

Where, oh, where are the eternity-conscious believers? Where are the souls white-hot for God because they fear His holy name and presence and so live with eternity's values in view?

LEONARD RAVENHILL, *Revival God's Way*

I ONCE HEARD ABOUT a pastor in a persecuted country who was thrown into solitary confinement for over a year because of his faith in Christ. Day after day, he crouched in a tiny cell with no light, no sound, and no human companionship. When he was finally released from prison, his body was weak, but his face was radiant and glowing. His Christian friends asked him, "How did you survive? What was it like?"

The frail pastor joyfully proclaimed, "It was like a dream come true—an entire year in the presence of Jesus!"

What an incredible statement! This man had spent more than 365 days in the most extreme isolation imaginable, with no earthly pleasures or comforts, and yet he was more than satisfied by the sweet soul-fellowship he had shared with his precious King. Jesus became, in reality, his everything. As a result, he didn't just survive those lonely months; he triumphed through them.

Imagine having all your pleasures and indulgences stripped away. No mall to shop at on the weekends. No coffee bars to make your favorite latte. No Facebook page to post on. No cell phone to text with. No Pinterest to browse. No Netflix or cable T.V. to entertain you. No gym membership to help you de-stress. No hair salons or spas to pamper you. No magazines or books to read. No chocolate desserts or whipped mocha Frappuccinos to enjoy.

Imagine losing all contact with those you love. No opportunity to see your husband or friends or children, or even to hear their voices over the phone. Imagine being completely by yourself, twenty-four hours a day.

Would Jesus be enough to satisfy you?

That piercing question changed my life many years ago. As I explained earlier, Eric and I were in full-time ministry, traveling, speaking, writing, and discipling. As an introvert, I was often burned out from this demanding lifestyle. I knew that I should be turning to Christ to revive my spirit, but after a long week of ministry work, I found myself wanting to take a break from spiritual things. When Friday nights came around, I finally had an excuse to engage in a little "me time." After working hard all week, it seemed perfectly acceptable to set aside my spiritual focus for a while and indulge in some frivolous activities.

Eric and I adopted a tradition of watching a movie every Friday night. It started out as a harmless and fun activity for us to do together, but soon we became addicted to zoning out in front of our big flat-screen. Movies and T.V. series became a way for us to escape from the intensity of ministry whenever we were feeling exhausted or discouraged. As our ministry roles became more challenging, we started watching movies or T.V. series several times a week. Whenever we felt especially burned out, we indulged in all-out movie marathons. (I remember one weekend getaway to the mountains during which we must have watched at least fifteen movies!)

At first, we had fairly high standards for which movies and shows we would watch—only G-rated and a small handful of PG-rated. But there were only so many family-friendly movies out there, and we had seen them all several times, so we lowered our standard to include PG-13 and even some R-rated movies, as long as there wasn't anything "really bad" in them, such as graphic sexual content. We excused a bit of profanity, crudeness, sensuality, and violence here and there. After all, we reasoned, it was still a lot better than what most people were watching.

Soon, ungodly messages, images, and attitudes no longer bothered us like they used to. But because the desensitization happened so gradually, we didn't even notice that we were growing spiritually dull. Spending so much time in front of movies and T.V. paved the way for other shallow, worldly pastimes to enter into my life. Trivial activities began to consume much of my free time. Instead of reading my Bible or inspiring Christian books, I often turned to novels and magazines. Instead of cultivating meaningful relationships with others, I wasted hours surfing the Internet for the latest fashion trends and beauty tips. Instead of taking time for personal worship or Scripture meditations, I downloaded the latest music from iTunes. Though I was in full-time ministry, I became more in tune with pop culture than with the Word of God.

Without even realizing it, I had exchanged an eternal focus for a temporal one. With my mouth, I proclaimed that the things of God were most important to me. But with my time and daily choices, I was placing much higher value on the things of the world.

When God walked Eric and me through that revival season I wrote about earlier, I began to change my daily habits to align with eternal priorities. I began spending time in His presence once again, praying, reading Scripture, and listening to worship music.

As I drew near to God, He drew near to me. Trivial pastimes and pop culture distractions were no longer attractive as I experienced the sweet presence of Jesus. I began to wonder how I ever could have sought satisfaction in anything outside of Him. Eric and I exchanged our movie nights for powerful times of prayer. Instead of mindlessly surfing the Internet during our spare time, we began studying Scripture and reading inspiring Christian biographies as we had done earlier in our marriage. We talked for hours about what God was doing in our hearts and what we were discovering in His Word. Our lives became centered around eternal things once more.

Something amazing happened as I began to spend my time on Christ-centered activities instead of frivolous ones. Jesus became my all in all, not just in theory but in reality. My relationship with Him began to satisfy all my needs. At the end of a long week of ministry, I no longer craved a mind-escape. I discovered that time with Jesus was the only thing that could refresh my soul. Prayer and time in God's Word gave me renewed energy and strength in a way movie marathons had never done. Temporal pastimes seemed meaningless compared to time spent on His priorities.

I began to experience the words of Psalm 16:11: "In Your presence is fullness of joy; at Your right hand are pleasures forevermore." By seeking pleasure through pop culture preoccupations, I had settled for a counterfeit peace and temporary joy. But as I built my life and my time around the eternal instead of the temporal, I discovered a true peace and lasting joy. My life has never been the same.

It's not that I haven't watched a movie or read a novel since that season of shifting my priorities. But my approach is far different than it used to be. I've learned not to turn to worldly entertainment to find the rest, joy, peace, rejuvenation, and fulfillment my soul needs. I have come to realize that the only place where I can find those things is at the feet of Jesus. If I turn elsewhere for comfort, I'm settling for a cheap counterfeit of the soul-level satisfaction that Jesus desires to give me. So now, whenever I'm deciding whether to spend my free time on a movie, novel, or similar activity, I ask myself these questions:

1. Is this activity distracting me from Christ or causing me to adopt the ungodly values of the world? If my answer is yes, then I shouldn't be doing it! John Tauler once said, "A pure heart is one to which all that is not of God is strange and jarring."[1] This statement has been a powerful reminder to keep me from becoming careless about the things that influence my heart and mind on a daily basis.

2. Am I turning to this activity for fulfillment instead of to Christ? If my answer is yes, then I need to reevaluate where I'm looking for satisfaction. There may not be anything particularly wrong with an activity, but if it's replacing my relationship with Christ, my priorities are off balance.

I still watch a family-friendly movie with my kids, read an edifying novel, or surf the Internet for decorating and cooking ideas from time to time. But I have learned that if any leisure activity is causing my relationship with Christ to suffer, then I need to reassess how I'm using my free time.

I have a long way to go to become as satisfied in Jesus as that imprisoned pastor was. And yet, the more I choose to come away from trivial things, the more I catch a glimpse of the joy and fulfillment that is possible when we spend our time on God's priorities instead of on the shallow distractions of the world. As Leonard Ravenhill said, "Entertainment is the devil's substitute for joy. The more joy you have in the Lord the less entertainment you need."[2]

MAKING THE EXCHANGE

God has entrusted us with the precious gift of time. Twenty-four hours in every day; seven days in every week; each day significant, each hour important, and each moment of value to God. How many of those moments are being spent on things that matter in light of eternity? Only when we are willing to give God the best hours of our day—rather than whatever is left after we have wasted most of our time on earthly things—will we experience vibrant intimacy with our heavenly King and become the set-apart women He has called us to be.

Here are some things you can do to exchange shallow pastimes for a Christ-centered lifestyle:

1. REMOVE *Time Wasters*

Many of us look at our daily schedules and can't see any available time for seeking God or sharing the Gospel with others. Yet often, our lives are filled with distractions and time wasters that take up far more of our free time than we realize. Social media, Internet surfing, phone chats, movies, and T.V. are a few of the most common culprits. Again, it's not that these mediums are always wrong in themselves, but if not put in their proper place, they can dominate our time and pull us away from building our lives around God's priorities. When we aren't guarded in these areas, we often waste our time on temporal things, without even realizing we are doing so.

Financial consultants often recommend that their clients keep a record of exactly what they are spending their money on. Often, as clients evaluate their spending habits, they are surprised to learn that they're spending far more in various categories than they would have guessed. The same principle applies to the way we spend our time. If asked to guess how much time you spend each day on social media, you might say, "Oh, probably a half hour or so." But if you were to set a timer each time you went on Facebook, Pinterest, or Twitter, you might be surprised to learn that you are spending far more time in those arenas than you had assumed you were.

Or how about texting and phone calls? I've never been much of a texter. But about a year ago, a friend of mine started texting me daily with various updates, comments, and ideas. I felt obligated to text her back whenever I had a pause in my work or family activities. After a few weeks, I began to realize that texting with my friend was taking up at least an hour of my day, and I knew it was not the best way for me to be spending that time. A lot of our texts were nothing more than idle chitchat. It was amazing how much of my time freed up once I eliminated the habit of unnecessary texting.

T.V. viewing is much the same; it can rob your precious time before you even know what's happening. You might sit down with the intent of watching one episode of your favorite show, but once that remote is in your hand, it's all too easy to click around from one show to the next for hours at a time. Eric and I have not had T.V. in our home for quite a few years. (We use our computer to watch family-friendly movies with our kids every now and then.) The peace that we've experienced by removing the distraction of T.V. has been palpable.

If you find yourself wondering where all your time has gone, consider keeping a diary of your daily activities, especially the things you spend your free time on. For a week or two, write down exactly how much time you spend on the phone, e-mailing, texting, on Facebook, on Pinterest, posting on Instagram, watching movies, channel surfing, reading magazines, and so on. Don't just guess at how much time you are spending on these things. Set a timer or monitor the clock as you do them, and write down the exact number of minutes or hours being spent on each activity. Then, prayerfully evaluate whether you need to cut or reduce any of these potential time wasters from your daily life.

Ask God to show you how to spend more of your time

on what is important. For instance, can you replace your nightly T.V. time with a regular prayer time instead? Can you dedicate some of your Facebook time to studying the Bible instead? Can you exchange your weekly movie night for encouraging a friend in need, or sharing Christ with one of your neighbors? Instead of letting leisure activities consume your weekend, could you spend some of that time serving the elderly, the poor, the imprisoned, or the refugees in your local community?

Yes, I realize that some of these suggestions might sound about as attractive as exchanging a Hawaiian vacation for a year of grueling factory work. But if you are willing to consecrate your time to Jesus Christ, you'll find a satisfaction far beyond what the distractions of the world can offer. When you experience the true and lasting fulfillment that comes from a lifestyle centered around God's priorities, you will no longer be content to settle for a counterfeit.

Remember, it's not that spending a little time on Facebook each day or watching an edifying movie now and then is sinful. The problem is devoting the majority of our free time to these things and allowing them to pull us away from a Christ-centered lifestyle. A good rule of thumb is this: Leisure activities should be an accent to our lives, not what we build our lives around! Ephesians 2:10 says that we are created to do the "good works" that God has prepared for each of us. Let's not miss out on the world-changing opportunities that God has in store for us each and every day.

The Bible says that a woman who builds her life around

the pursuit of selfish pleasure is "dead while she lives" (1 Tim. 5:6). What an incredibly poignant challenge to our souls. May we not waste the precious time that God has given us here on this earth!

David Wilkerson, the founder of Teen Challenge, was a young country preacher when God challenged him to make a dramatic change to his daily lifestyle. Every evening for a couple of hours he would watch T.V., partially to relax and partially to stay in touch with the culture. One night a strange thought entered his mind: What if he were to get rid of his T.V. and instead spend those two hours every night in prayer? He decided to try it. He sold his T.V., got on his knees, and from that point forward, incredible things began happening in his life and ministry. During David's nightly prayer times, God burdened his heart with the needs of the gang members in New York City. He felt God calling him to go and minister to these lost and hurting young people. Because he exchanged leisure time for prayer, David was sensitive to the Spirit of God guiding and directing him into the "good works" that God had prepared for him. He made a life-changing impact upon the gangs in New York City, offering them the hope of the Gospel and seeing some of the most hardened criminals give their lives to Jesus.[3]

I can't help wondering how we as Christian women could impact this world for eternity if we were willing to come away from time wasters and pursue Jesus Christ with all our heart, soul, mind, and strength.

2. GAIN AN *Eternal Focus*

God gave us a beautiful world to experience and delight in. Eric and I like to play tennis and go on bike rides together. I also enjoy sale-shopping, organizing, decorating, and going on fun outings with my kids. But even when I'm doing fun or recreational activities, God has challenged me to keep my focus centered on Him and His priorities for my life.

For example, I can approach an outing to the beach with my kids two different ways. If I am going on the outing to build meaningful relationships with my children, I'll spend my time helping them build sand castles, teaching them how to swim, or cheering them on as they play and explore. Though I may be doing something recreational, my focus is still on something of eternal value—cultivating meaningful relationships with my kids.

On the other hand, if I am going to the beach for the sole purpose of lounging around while reading a fashion magazine and working on my tan, I'll ignore my kids and indulge in some "me time." One attitude is pleasing to God; the other caters to selfish pleasure.

As you go about your daily life, prayerfully examine the motives behind *why* you spend time doing the things that you do. When evaluating any activity, ask yourself these questions: Am I doing this for selfish reasons, or Christ-honoring ones? Is this activity frivolous, or does it serve a higher purpose?

Here are some ways you can tell whether something has eternal value:

- It causes you to draw closer to Jesus Christ and/or learn more about Him.
- It builds meaningful relationships with people God has put in your life.
- It helps you bless others and assists you in sharing the love of Christ with them.
- It helps you become better equipped for the things God has called you to.
- It leaves you peacefully refreshed instead of agitated and distracted.
- It bears "good fruit" instead of "bad fruit" in your life (see Gal. 5:19-23).

To evaluate whether your choices are serving God's purposes for your life, write down the specific things that you know God has called you to, and then compare your daily activities against those things. During this season of my life, I know that God has called me to cultivate my relationship with Him, serve my husband and children, be a keeper of my home, minister to the weak, and encourage women in biblical femininity. When I'm evaluating my activities, I look at each of my pastimes in light of whether they are assisting me in those priorities. Reading a book on how to bless and serve my husband? Yes! Spending an hour chatting on the phone while my kids run wildly around the house? No! E-mailing a friend who is in need of encouragement? Yes! Texting about trivial things throughout the day? No!

The Bible says that even the small areas of our lives, like

eating and drinking, should be done for His glory and not our own selfish pleasure (see 1 Cor. 10:31). When you allow your daily activities to serve God's purposes for your life rather than your own, you will begin to gain an eternal focus in everything you do.

3. RETHINK *"Me Time"*

At times during His life, Jesus needed rest and refueling. The Bible describes several occasions when He periodically withdrew from the demands of the crowds and the intensity of His ministry. But He didn't lounge on the beach or turn to entertainment to find the rest and new strength He needed. Instead, Jesus went alone to a mountain to pray or rose up early in the morning to spend time in God's presence (see Mk. 1:35; 6:46).

Jesus carried more weight on His shoulders than any of us can ever even imagine. Yet He knew that the only way to gain strength for the battles He was called to fight was to spend time alone with God.

As busy women, we often find ourselves in need of rest, perspective, and new strength. It's tempting to try to do things that have no eternal value, yet will distract us temporarily.

Always remember, when we take time alone to refresh and refuel, it should flow from a motive of becoming even stronger and more equipped to serve Jesus Christ, not simply to escape from the responsibilities of serving and godly living. Certainly there is nothing wrong with doing practical things in order to refuel and recharge. A long walk, a refreshing bike ride, an hour journaling outside in God's creation, an encouraging chat with a trusted friend, or a family vacation can be wonderful ways to gain clearer perspective. But it's important not to give in to the voice that whispers, "You deserve some self-indulgence right now. Forget about everyone else. Put your spiritual life on hold for a while. Take time for *you!*"

Over the past several years in ministry and motherhood, I have found that the best "me time" is actually not "me time" at all, but "God time." Prayer journaling, worship, and reading Christian biographies produce far more lasting refreshment to my soul than an hour on social media ever could. Remember, there should be no area of our lives that is exclusively ours. Rather, every area of our lives should be exclusively God's.

When we say no to personal indulgences in order to say yes to time in God's presence, we find all of the lasting joy, peace, and strength we need in Him.

Next time you feel like you are in need of some "me time," take a moment to consider what will refresh your soul. Run to the feet of Jesus instead of to the comforts of this world. You'll catch a glimpse of what that imprisoned pastor experienced when everything else was stripped away, and Jesus became his everything.

4. AVOID IDLE *Chatter*

Proverbs 14:23 tells us that "idle chatter leads only to poverty." When we waste time and energy on chitchat, we end up spiritually impoverished. And yet, it is all too easy to waste much of our time on idle conversations (either face-to-face or via phone and computer).

During Paul's evangelistic journeys in the book of Acts, he came upon a group of Athenians who "spent their time in nothing else but either to tell or to hear some new thing" (Acts 17:21). Though at first these people expressed an interest in hearing Paul's message, only a few of them embraced the life-changing Truth of Christ. Second Timothy 2:16 says, "Shun profane and idle babblings, for they will increase to more ungodliness." The term *idle babbling* means "empty discussion, discussion of vain and useless matters."[4] What a perfect description of much of our communication! Facebook comments, Twitter, Pinterest boards, and even blogs can often be breeding grounds for idle chatter, emotional ramblings, showing off of wit and personality, and exalting our own thoughts and opinions instead of God's thoughts and opinions.

This kind of *idle babbling* is the opposite of the godly, fruitful, eternally focused communication that we are called to as Christians. Romans 14:19 says, "Let us pursue the things which make for peace and the things by which one may edify another."

The Greek word for *edification* means "the act of one who promotes another's growth in Christian wisdom, piety, happiness, holiness."[5] In other words, if you don't have something important, edifying, and God-honoring to say, then don't say it (or post it)! Jesus said in Matthew 12:36, "Every idle word men may speak, they will give account of it in the day of judgment." With all of today's modern technology, it's so easy to say or write meaningless words without even thinking about it. But Jesus says we must weigh each word we say (and write) in light of eternity.

If you choose to blog, text, tweet, or post on Pinterest, Instagram, or Facebook, your goal should be to edify your readers, to build up others' faith in Jesus Christ and encourage them spiritually through what you are sharing, or to bless your friends and family members and remind them of your love for them. If your online communications serve no eternal purpose, they become nothing more than time wasters and distractions, not only in your own life, but in the lives of those you are conversing with.

One of the most dangerous things about Facebook, Pinterest, and personal blogs is the temptation to idolize the "following" that we gain through these mediums. Instead of looking to Christ for our confidence, security, and fulfillment, we become consumed with how many "likes" we have on our Facebook page, how many people follow our Pinterest boards, or how many subscribers we have on our blog. When our motive is to maintain or build up a following, it can be tempting to post merely for the sake of posting something and getting people to listen to us. But meaningless chatter always draws attention to *us*, instead of to Jesus Christ.

A great way to figure out whether the words you are posting, tweeting, blogging, or texting have eternal value is to ask the questions, "Do these words point people to Jesus Christ and reflect His nature? Do they serve any higher purpose other than to fill space and sound interesting? Do they honor God, or do they esteem the shallow things of this world?" If your words are hollow and meaningless, then it's better not to say (or write) them.

If digital idle chatter has become an unhealthy pattern in your life, prayerfully consider taking a season away from all the outlets (blogs, social media, and so on) that seem to pull you into that habit. Use that time instead for prayer and worship, serving someone in need, encouraging people in your daily life, or reaching out to someone who is lonely. This habit might seem difficult to give up at first, but if you ask God for the grace to make this exchange, He will be faithful to give you the strength you need. And just like all the other areas we have been discussing in this chapter, once you discover the "real thing," you will no longer be satisfied with a counterfeit.

To become the set-apart women God has called us to be, we must remember that this world is not our home. Each moment we have on this earth is a gift from heaven, a beautiful opportunity to live out the sacred, set-apart calling Christ has placed upon our lives. May we not waste this precious time that God has given us! Let us ask Him for the grace to turn our attention away from distractions and onto the things that matter most to Him. May we live lives that proclaim, "Nothing else matters to me but the things that are eternal!"

LET'S TALK ABOUT IT

🗨 *Group Study and Discussion*

1. **READ 1 TIMOTHY 5:6.** What does it mean to live for eternity instead of for temporal pleasure? What does a woman's daily life look like when she chooses an eternal focus over a temporal one?

2. **READ EPHESIANS 5:15-16.** What are some of the most common time wasters in our society? When we fall prey to these pitfalls, how does it affect our relationship with Christ?

TAKE IT DEEPER

📖 *Personal Study and Reflection*

READ: PROVERBS 31:27

REFLECT: Am I choosing idleness and frivolity over purposeful time in God's presence and in serving others? If so, am I willing to exchange a temporal focus for an eternal one? What areas of my daily life need to change in order for me to do so?

READ: PSALM 16:11

REFLECT: Have I been settling for counterfeit peace and joy? Am I willing to find my joy, peace, satisfaction, and rest in Christ instead of in trivial distractions? What changes do I feel He is asking me to make in order to do this?

CHAPTER FIVE

Incorruptible Beauty

Exchanging Drama and Gossip for a Quiet Spirit

Aspire to lead a quiet life, to mind your own business.

1 THESSALONIANS 4:11

The incorruptible beauty of a gentle and quiet spirit . . . is very precious in the sight of God.

1 PETER 3:4

If I can easily discuss the shortcomings and the sins of any . . . if I can in any way slight another in conversation, or even in thought, then I know nothing of Calvary love.

AMY CARMICHAEL, *If*

God never gives us discernment in order that we may criticize, but that we may intercede.

OSWALD CHAMBERS

WHEN I WAS NINE, I dreamed of becoming a detective just like Nancy Drew. My best friend, Sarah, and I became the self-appointed mystery-solvers of our suburban neighborhood. We had all the gear: walkie-talkies (these only worked if we were within five feet of each other, but at least they looked cool), dark sunglasses (so no one would recognize us), and a notebook in which we carefully recorded all the suspicious activity we observed ("Mr. Jones from next door got his mail today—and he acted kind of sneaky about it"). We were ready to take a serious bite out of crime. We imagined being the first child detectives to win medals for our shrewd outsmarting of all the local "bad guys."

The problem was, there were no bad guys around. At least, none that we could find. No matter how many stakeouts we set up, nothing sinister ever happened on our boring, predictable street. We realized that if we wanted any mystery-solving excitement, we'd have to create it for ourselves. So we launched an adventure called "The Mystery of the X." The name was inspired when we noticed a bright orange X spray painted on the sidewalk. Sarah's dad told us that the X was there to mark the spot where electrical wires were buried under the street. But we knew there had to be more to the story. "I bet it's a clue that leads to the bad guys' secret hideout!" I whispered to Sarah. She was captivated by the intrigue, and from that day on, we were embroiled in an exciting mission to find the criminals' hub.

"I found a grocery store receipt lying on the ground!" Sarah would tell me. "It's a clue!"

"Yes, and I just found another orange X down the street," I would chime in. "That's another clue!"

Our imaginations ran wild. Every person we encountered became a character in our unfolding drama. Every car that drove onto our street became part of the story.

"I bet that lady in the red van is a bank robber. She looks like she's up to something."

"Yes, you're right! And I think that guy with the blue jacket is her secret partner in crime. I bet he has all the stolen money hidden somewhere in his house."

The Mystery of the X kept us occupied for several months. It was filled with endless excitement, adventure, and imaginary peril. I cannot remember exactly how it ended, whether we actually solved the mystery or simply decided that we'd never catch the bad guys after all. But what I vividly recall is how skilled Sarah and I were at inventing stories, making up clues, and building an alternate reality that was so much better than real life.

My ability to create drama was harmless and innocent enough at the age of nine. But a few years down the road, my drama-making skill had morphed into something very different.

"I saw Tracy flirting with Matt today," I squawked into the phone one Friday when I was fourteen. "She's probably cheating on Nathan. We should talk to Kelly about it and see if she knows anything." Thus the theatrical Tracy/Matt/

Nathan love triangle unfolded out of thin air. And it took up all my time, thoughts, and energy for about a month.

When that drama subsided, I was quick to find another one. "I'm so worried about Amber. She's really depressed since Julie stopped being her friend. I'm the only person she will talk to about it. Last night she was crying on the phone with me for two hours. I'm going to write Julie a letter about it."

Who needed the Mystery of the X when so much real-life drama swirled around me? It was like living in a soap opera; there were always couples breaking up, friends getting mad at each other, and interesting love triangles forming. All I had to do was plant myself right in the middle of them, sometimes stir things up through strategic gossip, and voila! Another great drama would emerge. When God got ahold of my life, drama was one of the first areas He began to put His finger on. The more I studied His Word and His nature, the more I realized that my thoughts and emotions were to be centered on Him, not on the latest gossip or romantic saga from my circle of friends. But because these habits had been ingrained in me for many years, this was easier said than done.

As I grew older, I always felt I needed to be in the know, at the center of the latest rift or relational issue. I wanted to be the one that girls cried to on the phone, the one that everyone shared their secrets with, and the one who noticed romantic flings forming before anyone else did. I wanted to be at the center of all the action. And if no excitement existed, I knew how to create it, just like when I was nine years old with my detective's notebook.

But God was saying, "Learn to live a quiet life—one that is built around Me—and mind your own business. I alone can fulfill you at the deepest level. Life with Me is a grand adventure; getting caught up in human drama is a waste of your precious time."

So I asked God to retrain me. I began learning how to pull away from the drama, shut my ears to the gossip, and ignore the latest "he said, she said" news. And surprisingly, it was incredibly liberating.

As I began to spend my time and energy building intimacy with Christ, I learned how to withdraw from friendships that were based on nothing but ridiculous drama. And I learned how to build meaningful friendships that were centered upon Jesus Christ.

I discovered that a Christ-centered life was far more exciting than any contrived human drama. Every day with Him became a great exploration, solving the beautiful mystery of His nature, His pattern, His ways. Unlike a temporary romance saga or neighborhood mystery, discovering His Truth knows no end, and it only gets more exciting and intriguing as time goes on.

DRAWN TO DRAMA

Now that I'm an adult, I've realized that women don't need to be in a high-school clique or childhood detective club to get sucked into a vortex of social drama. Simply being female makes us intrigued with human dynamics. Some women seek to satisfy their thirst for drama through pop-culture enticements, wasting hours on romance novels, Hollywood gossip magazines, or reality TV shows, preferring the thrill of manufactured sagas above the unromantic dullness of everyday life. Others plant themselves in the middle of every relational conflict that swirls around their churches or social circles, gaining satisfaction from being "in the know" about everyone's grievances, misunderstandings, and tiffs.

All too often, if we can't find a good drama to get caught up in, we'll create one through strategically positioned words of gossip, dealt out at just the right moment in just the right way. You know, the kind of conversation that starts out with, "I'm very concerned about so-and-so—we really need to be praying for her, because I've noticed that she always does such and such." (Followed by a detailed play-by-play of everything "so-and-so" is doing wrong, and all the reasons we should be concerned about her.) Typically there is little praying and quite a bit of "spiritualized gossiping" that takes place in these scenarios.

Women's prayer gatherings and coffee dates can turn into gossip sessions if we are not on our guard against the pitfall of drama.

In 2 Corinthians 12:20, Paul wrote about his concern over one of the churches:

> For I am afraid that when I come I may not find
> you as I want you to be. . . . I fear that there may
> be discord, jealousy, fits of rage, selfish ambition,
> slander, gossip, arrogance and disorder. (NIV)

Just think about how perfectly this describes the state of affairs in a typical sorority house, clique of high-school girlfriends, and many women's social, church, or family dynamics.

Drama is destructive. Not only does it eat away our precious time and energy, but it also erodes our intimacy with Christ. We cannot seek our King with an undivided heart while caught up in the "he said, she said" hearsay that swirls around us. We cannot glorify Jesus Christ when we spend our words, thoughts, and emotions on human drama.

Remember Rachel Lynde in the classic story *Anne of Green Gables*? Rachel was the nosy neighbor of Matthew and Marilla. This fictional character paints a vivid picture of what happens when our obsession with drama isn't curbed. We become prying old gossips, constantly "meddling in other people's affairs," as Anne Shirley would say, and wreaking havoc in relationships all around us. There is nothing noble or beautiful about this kind of womanhood. It's pesky, annoying, intrusive, and self-centered. God warns us against this behavior in 1 Timothy 5:13: "At the same time they also learn to be idle, as they go around from house to house; and not merely idle, but also gossips and busybodies, talking about things not proper to mention" (NASB).

The good news is, even though we are prone to drama and gossip, God has a refreshingly different pattern upon which we can build our femininity—the incorruptible beauty of a quiet spirit: "Do not let your adornment be merely outward . . . rather let it be the hidden person of the heart, with the incorruptible beauty of a gentle and quiet spirit, which is very precious in the sight of God" (1 Pet. 3:3-4).

Have you ever seen a woman who minds her own business? She protects the "hidden person of the heart"; she guards the sacred secrets of her soul. She exudes a peaceful, unwavering gentleness of spirit. Whether she is naturally quiet or has a vibrant personality, she does not allow her emotions to lead her actions. She is busy about her Father's work; she finds her delight in Him. Such a woman is truly a delight, both to those around her and to the heart of her God.

When we engage in the consecrated life God has called us to, we can be sure that our lives will be anything but dull! A life centered around Jesus Christ leads to many incredible heavenly adventures and God-scripted expeditions as we follow in His footsteps and do the work He calls us to do. But if we seek excitement and intrigue outside of Him, we settle for a counterfeit of the thrilling journey He has for us.

MAKING THE EXCHANGE

To become set-apart women, God says we are to forsake drama and gossip for the incorruptible beauty of a quiet spirit. The following principles from God's Word can help us make this all-important exchange.

1. *Pursue a* "QUIET AND PEACEABLE LIFE"

First Timothy 2:2 exhorts us to "lead a quiet and peaceable life in all godliness and honesty" (KJV). The phrase *quiet and peaceable* denotes a tranquil heart and mind, at rest from fretting, worrying, arguing, and—most especially—barging into other people's business. We are told in Hebrews 12:14 that we should "make every effort to live in peace with everyone" (NIV), and again in Romans 12:18, "if it is possible, as far as it depends on you, live at peace with everyone" (NIV).

Our two young daughters, Harper and Avonlea, both have the tendency to be drama queens. When Harper doesn't get her way, she will often sulk and sniff as crocodile tears run down her chubby cheeks. Moodiness is her choice weapon for creating drama. Avonlea (Avy), on the other hand, does the opposite. When something happens that she doesn't like, she tends to make a huge emotional scene. Taking center stage is her method of choice for creating drama.

Both Harper and Avy understand the word *drama*. Whenever we see them use their playacting skills in a manipulative way, we say, "No drama!" Those two little words are a warning that they'd better get some self-control over their emotions or reap some serious consequences.

The secret to living a quiet and peaceable life is not allowing our emotions to lead us. By God's grace it *is* possible not to overreact when things don't go our way, or to get offended when someone is insensitive, or to allow selfish desires to rule our attitudes. Rather, we can choose to control our reactions and submit our emotions to the Spirit of God. Whenever the temptation to react emotionally arises, tell yourself, "No drama!" and choose the path of peace. Instead of pouting, sulking, lashing out, or ignoring someone who is irritating you, try praying for that person instead. Even better, say or do something kind to them.

Proverbs 15:1 tells us that "a soft answer turns away wrath, but a harsh word stirs up anger." Following this simple yet brilliant advice will enable you to lead a tranquil life. It may take a bit of practice and a lot of supernatural grace, but it leads to a beautiful, peace-filled existence that brings glory to our King.

2. MIND YOUR OWN *Business*

First Thessalonians 4:11 exhorts us to mind our own business. Most women are acutely interested in the small details of other people's lives. We can spend hours hearing all the particulars of so-and-so's wedding or the birth of so-and-so's baby. We can cry tears of joy when we hear about how a guy proposed to his future wife, even if we've never met the couple. We want to know all about the wedding colors and clothing or the baby's height and weight, and we want to relive every emotion felt and expressed throughout the entire experience. Most men, however, are fine to just hear the basics. "So-and-so got married yesterday" is about all they care to be told.

A woman's love for small details can be a beautiful thing; when submitted to the Spirit of God, it can add romance, sparkle, and beauty to everyday life. It enables us to "rejoice with those who rejoice" (Ro. 12:15) in a special and meaningful way. It helps us be sensitive and empathetic listeners when someone is struggling with something.

But our love for knowing details can also lead to trouble.

It's fine to be excited about somebody getting married or having a baby. And there's nothing wrong with celebrating the wonderful things that happen in other people's lives or with listening when someone is hurting. Yet when we seek to know everything about everyone, to find out every detail about the ups and downs of people's lives, and hear all the nitty-gritty of every little saga they go through, we quickly become the "busybody" warned against in 1 Peter 4:15: "But let none of you suffer as a murderer, a thief, an evildoer, or as a busybody in other people's matters."

Modern technology makes it easier than ever to be a busybody. If not used properly, Twitter or texting can easily put all the details of our personal lives on display for others to see, or place all the minutia of everyone else's life right in front of our noses, all day long. If we build our lives around digital drama, we'll spend our days consumed with gossip, chatter, and meddling in other people's business. To mind your own business means to focus on your own relationship with Jesus Christ and on what He has called you to, instead of planting yourself in the middle of other people's lives.

Being a busybody can become an addiction that sneaks into our lives under the banner of "helping people" or "being a listening ear." It may start with a desire to help someone, but if we are not guarded we may soon find we love the thrill of "hearing all the details." And our focus shifts away from Jesus to the latest saga between this person and that person. Like all sinful habits, this must be broken by the supernatural, enabling grace of God.

Ask Him to show you the practical steps that you need to take in order to mind your own business. And remember—when in doubt, walk away. It's always better to spend time in the presence of your King than frittering away the hours on your computer or cell phone.

3. WORK WITH YOUR *Own Hands*

The same verse that exhorts us to mind our own business also tells us to work with our own hands (see 1 Thess. 4:11). If we pour ourselves into valuable work for the kingdom of God or into cultivating our relationship with Christ, we are much less likely to spend our energy on gossip or drama.

Titus 2:4-5 exhorts older women to train younger women to "love their husbands, to love their children, to be discreet, chaste, homemakers, good, obedient to their own husbands, that the word of God may not be blasphemed." And Proverbs 31:27 describes a godly woman as one who "watches over the ways of her household, and does not eat the bread of idleness."

This is the opposite of today's T.V. dramas and reality shows, in which women are consumed with self-centered sagas and obsessing about who did this and who said that. Hollywood may make such femininity look enticing. But God says it's a path that leads to death and emptiness (see 1 Tim. 5:6).

Whether married or single, we are to be busy about God's work. First Corinthians 7:34 says, "The unmarried woman cares about the things of the Lord, that she may be holy both in body and in spirit."

No matter the season of our lives, we are never to live

selfishly or idly. Every day, millions of people are dying without Jesus Christ. Countless orphans, foster-care children, elderly people, prisoners, and refugees are in desperate need of God's love. Are we being Christ's hands and feet to them, or are we too busy watching the newest episode of our favorite reality show or pursuing the latest banter on Twitter or Facebook? Are we showcasing the incorruptible beauty of a Christ-consumed heart, or are we too busy gossiping with our girlfriends?

Working with our own hands, doing things for others, is a great cure for drama obsession. When we invest our time and energy into the things that really matter, we soon find that we have all the excitement, fulfillment, and adventure we could ever want or need. When we spend our time and energy training our children in the ways of God, ministering to the needs of our husbands, and doing other Kingdom work such as rescuing orphans, feeding the hungry, opening our homes to foster-care children, practicing hospitality, and sharing the Gospel with the unsaved, we find we have little time to waste on the latest church gossip or chitchat on Twitter. And we will no longer crave counterfeit human drama in order to find excitement or fulfillment, because we will be experiencing the *real* adventure and excitement of a God-scripted life! (We'll discuss practical ways to serve others in chapter 10.)

No matter what our natural bent, by God's grace, each of us can be set free from the snares of drama and gossip, and endued with His strength to follow a different pattern. All we must do is fall at His feet in surrender and allow Him to transform us into a reflection of His beauty. Remember, "faithful is He who calls you, and He also will bring it to pass" (1 Thess. 5:24, NASB).

LET'S TALK ABOUT IT

Group Study and Discussion

1. **READ 1 PETER 3:3-4.** What is the difference between a busybody and a woman with a quiet spirit? When we choose a quiet spirit, how does it impact our relationship with Christ?

2. **READ 1 TIMOTHY 5:13.** Why are gossip and drama so dangerous, both to our own soul and to those around us?

TAKE IT DEEPER

Personal Study and Reflection

READ: PROVERBS 16:28

REFLECT: Have I been unguarded with my tongue? Have I hurt others by listening to or speaking gossip? Am I willing to repent of this sin and allow God to cultivate a quiet spirit within me? (If yes, take a moment to do this.)

READ: 1 THESSALONIANS 4:11

REFLECT: Have I been looking to human drama for excitement instead of to my relationship with Christ? Am I willing to lead a quiet life, to mind my own business and find my adventure in my relationship with Him instead? What habits in my life must change in order for me to do this?

CHAPTER SIX

He Must Increase

Exchanging Self-Promotion for Humility

Do nothing out of selfish ambition or vain conceit.

PHILIPPIANS 2:3, NIV

He must increase, but I must decrease.

JOHN 3:30

Christianity says, "The end of all being is the glory of God."
Humanism says, "The end of all being is the happiness of man."
And one born in Hell, the deification of man. And the other
was born in Heaven, the glorification of God!

PARIS REIDHEAD, "Ten Shekels and a Shirt"

Till we are poor in spirit, Christ is never precious. Before we see
our own wants, we never see Christ's worth.

THOMAS WATSON, "The Beatitudes: An Exposition of Matthew 5:1-12"

SOMETIME DURING my early teens, I decided I wanted to be a famous Christian singer. I think it was attending a Christian concert with my youth group that first planted the idea in my mind. A beautiful young woman onstage, decked out in a dazzling outfit, belting out catchy tunes in front of thousands of adoring fans under a canopy of stunning lights and smoke—who wouldn't want that kind of attention and applause?

I'd been singing and performing for most of my life. People (mostly biased family members) were always telling me I had musical talent and that I was a natural performer. I loved being onstage. From playing the lead angel in the church Christmas musical, to my many (rather tedious) piano recitals, I always felt a rush of excitement when I heard others applauding me.

Even at a young age, I tuned in to society's exhortations to "go for your dreams!" and "do what makes you happy!" I came to believe that one of the highest ideals I could achieve was the pursuit of my own happiness. Nearly every magazine cover, billboard ad, Disney movie, and commercial on T.V. encouraged me toward this mind-set.

Having my musical talent noticed and appreciated made me happy. So, at the age of thirteen, I told my parents that my dream was to become a Christian musician when I grew up. Naturally, they wanted to help me reach my goal. They signed me up for voice lessons, took me to countless musical auditions and songwriting competitions, encouraged me to participate in every church or school play that came along, and even hired a producer to help me write and record my own music. Along the way, all of the music industry experts we met offered us plenty of tips on how I could make it in the music biz or get discovered by a talent scout from Nashville.

"Get a professional photo shoot done," one music producer told me. "It will help build your image. Have some eight-by-ten glossies printed, and give them to every music professional you meet."

"Record a demo album," another producer told me. "Put your best songs on it, and have it ready to give to anyone you meet who is connected with the music industry."

Others told me: "Write an impressive bio. List all the competitions you've won, the awards you've received, and the musicals you've starred in. Make it sound larger than life."

The more I got involved in the Christian music industry, the more I kept hearing the message, "Promote yourself, promote yourself, promote yourself!" I was even told that self-promotion was the only way I could be a good steward of the talent God had given me.

At fourteen, I attended a national conference for aspiring Christian musicians. Thousands of people from all over the country came to learn how to "get discovered" by a record company. I quickly realized I wasn't the only one trying to promote myself and my musical talent. Nearly every person I met mentioned how they had talked with a producer who showed a lot of interest in their demo album, or how they had won a songwriting competition that had given them a lot of exposure, or how they had met a famous artist, which gave them a foot in the door. Yes, there were a handful of aspiring artists at the conference who weren't as concerned about being noticed as they were with leading people to Christ through their musical gifts. But for the most part, the Christian music world was a subculture based upon self-marketing and personal ambition.

No one talked about the fact that this "promote yourself" mantra wasn't exactly a scriptural idea. We were convinced that we were seeking to honor God with our music skills. Self-promotion was just a necessary step to gaining the platform we needed. How else would we ever get famous enough to wow the crowds with our talents and then "give all the glory to God"?

A few years later, God began gently shining His searchlight of conviction upon this area of my life. As I drew nearer to Jesus Christ and embraced a life of surrender to Him, I awakened to the fact that my musical pursuits were self-focused. None of my ambitions had truly been for His glory, but for my own desire to be appreciated, applauded, and recognized. The more I studied Scripture, the more I came to realize that the Christian life was not supposed to be about self-promotion, but self-denial.

I began to see that if I wanted to bring glory to God through my music, it would not involve trying to impress people with my talent and then mentioning God's name as an afterthought. To serve Christ with an undivided heart, I had to let go of my desire to be center stage. I had to exchange my dream for personal glory for a new dream: bringing *Him* glory in every area of my life and pointing people's eyes to Jesus, even if no one ever noticed me at all.

This was not an easy exchange to make. But as I asked Him for the grace and strength to obey, I found amazing peace in withdrawing from my self-promoting lifestyle and laying my personal ambitions at His feet.

THE LURE OF SELF-PROMOTION

You don't have to be an aspiring musician to fall into the trap of self-promotion. Most of us have an intrinsic desire to be seen, noticed, admired, and appreciated. What little girl doesn't dream of being a Disney princess, waltzing into the ballroom in a gorgeous dress and dazzling everyone with her beauty and charm? As we grow older, our desire to be recognized and applauded spills into many other areas of life. Whether it's in pursuit of a guy, a career, a ministry opportunity, or a bigger social-media following, we can easily become preoccupied with drawing attention toward ourselves instead of humbly pointing people to Jesus Christ. In fact, we often believe it is our responsibility to promote ourselves in order to gain the things we desire. We're told:

"Want to find your future husband? Promote yourself! Put together an impressive Facebook page. Include numerous photos of yourself in various outfits to show off your look, and post witty comments to show how great your personality is. Join an online dating service and put together a beautiful profile so guys can be impressed with who you are. Go to every singles' group you can find, and make sure all the available Christian men see what a great catch you are!"

Or,

"Want to be successful in your career? Promote yourself! Constantly drop hints about your importance and take offense if you aren't recognized for the work you do. Don't waste your time with the little obscure jobs that no one else will see. Only do the impressive and important tasks that will get you noticed. Make a name for yourself so that you don't get overlooked!"

Or,

"Feel called to start a ministry? Promote yourself! Get an agent, come up with a catchy name for your message, and find your unique niche in the Christian world. Get yourself out there. Look for opportunities to get noticed, and put yourself in front of people over and over again, until you gain the recognition and credibility you deserve!"

Messages regarding the need for self-promotion are easy to buy into, because they sound so wise and logical. And as Christians, we often spiritualize the idea of self-promotion. After all, the more successful and popular we become, the better Christian witnesses we will be, right? But surprisingly, that's not God's pattern at all.

A DIFFERENT WAY TO MEASURE SUCCESS

At the peak of John the Baptist's ministry, Jesus also started baptizing, and people began coming more to Jesus than to John. Disturbed by this trend, John's followers told him,

ild, He is baptizing, and all are coming to Him!"
3:26). They must have felt jealous on behalf of John,
inking, *Why is John suddenly getting overlooked? People aren't
noticing him as much, now that Jesus is around. John should do
something to promote himself and his ministry.*

And yet John knew that his sacred commission was to
make Jesus, not himself, known to the world. He told his
followers, "I am only the friend of the Bridegroom; not the
Bridegroom Himself; when the Bridegroom is seen, my joy
is complete" (Jn. 3:29, author's paraphrase). And then John
made a profound statement: "He must increase, but I must
decrease" (Jn. 3:30). What an amazing attitude! John's primary concern was getting out of the way so that Jesus could
be seen. He knew that if he tried to take center stage, Jesus
would not receive the glory that He deserved.

The same is true in our own lives. When we try to be seen
and applauded, Jesus fades into the background, and people
look at *us*, not Him. But when we focus on getting out of
the way and pointing others to Him, He receives the glory
He deserves.

This doesn't mean we can never cultivate the unique talents and strengths that He has given us. It is certainly possible
to use our gifts to glorify God (in fact, that is why He gave
them to us in the first place!). But first, we must ask some
critical questions: Am I doing this for His glory or for my
own applause? When people see this part of my life, are they
drawn closer to Jesus, or are they merely impressed with me?

If we are more concerned with what others think of us than

with what they think of Jesus, then we have not learned how to be a faithful friend of the Bridegroom, as John the Baptist was. If we are pursuing our dreams in order to get what we want out of life rather than to lead others to the Source of true life, we are missing a crucial part of Christianity.

Jesus said, "If anyone would come after me, let him deny himself and take up his cross and follow me" (Mt. 16:24, ESV). The word *deny* here means "to forget one's self and lose sight of one's own interests." What an incredibly different message from the "take what you deserve" notion that our culture promotes! Jesus says that in order to follow Him, we must lay down all pursuits of self-glory and seek His glory alone.

When Jackie Pullinger was a young woman, she left all her dreams and personal pursuits in order to share the hope of Christ among the destitute and dying in the Walled City of Hong Kong, a dangerous and poverty-stricken part of the city where police were scarce and crime was rampant. One day, not long after she arrived, she was walking down a filthy street and saw people openly smoking heroin. They were longtime drug addicts—their bodies shriveled and wasting away, their souls lost and despairing. No one knew their names or cared whether they lived or died. As the young woman watched the heartbreaking scene in front of her, she silently said to God, "It would be worth my whole life if You would use me to help just one of them." Although she had her whole life ahead of her, Jackie was ready to leave it all behind just to lead one old man to Jesus Christ.[1]

Such a self-sacrificing attitude might at first seem foolish to our logical minds. If we could speak to Jackie, we might say, "You are such a bright and beautiful young woman; don't throw away your life for the sake of one old man! Surely there are better ways—bigger ways—for you to make an impact in God's kingdom!"

But God doesn't measure success the way we do. Mary of Bethany poured out her most priceless possession upon the feet of Jesus without applause, recognition, or fanfare, and some thought it was a waste. Yet Jesus said, in essence, "What she has done for me is a picture of the Gospel itself" (see Mk. 14:3-9). The apostle Paul had loads of accomplishments and accolades that he could have leveraged to gain a bigger platform for his ministry. But only when he was willing to consider his earthly achievements worthless and become a fool for Christ's sake was he truly effective as a witness of the Gospel (see Phil. 3:7-8; 1 Cor. 1:27-28). Jesus said that if we cling to our lives, we will lose them, but if we are willing to give up our lives for His sake, we will find true lives (see Mt. 10:39).

Instead of striving to be noticed and appreciated, we are to take an entirely different posture into every area of our lives, one of humility and self-denial. Whether we are recognized and applauded or disregarded and overlooked, it should make no difference to us. A woman who has taken up her cross to follow Christ only cares about knowing Him and making Him known.

Amy Carmichael understood this. She wrote, "If my thoughts revolve around myself . . . then I know nothing of Calvary love. . . . If I cannot in honest happiness take the second place (or twentieth) . . . then I know nothing of Calvary love."[2]

We've been conditioned to believe that self-promotion is right and good, but as set-apart women, we are called by God to forget ourselves and let all our own interests become swallowed up in Him. We are not to seek the highest place, but the lowest one.

Nowhere in Scripture is this better illustrated than when Jesus humbly took the position of a lowly servant to wash his disciples' feet: "Jesus, knowing that the Father had given all things into His hands, and that He had come from God and was going to God, rose from supper and laid aside His garments, took a towel and girded Himself" (Jn. 13:3-4).

"He took a towel," wrote Amy Carmichael. "The Lord of glory did that. Is it the bondservant's business to say which work is large and which is small, which is unimportant and which is worth doing?"[3]

Jesus knew exactly who He was—the King over heaven and earth, with all things under His feet. Yet He willingly humbled Himself and took the lowest position, one of a servant who washed the dirt and mire from the disciples' feet.

Following this astonishing act, He said, "If I then, your Lord and Teacher, have washed your feet, you also ought to wash one another's feet. For I have given you an example, that you should do as I have done to you" (Jn. 13:14-15). Jesus' life was a picture of this kind of humility, of willingly choosing the lowest place rather than the highest one. And

He lived this out as an example for us, that we should follow in His steps (see 1 Pet. 2:21).

Paul reminds us, "Let nothing be done through selfish ambition or conceit, but in lowliness of mind let each esteem others better than himself. . . . Let this mind be in you which was also in Christ Jesus, who, being in the form of God . . . made Himself of no reputation, taking the form of a bondservant, and coming in the likeness of men. . . . He humbled Himself and became obedient to the point of death" (Phil. 2:3-8).

Imagine the freedom of being unconcerned whether people appreciated your unique talents, personality, or acts of service. Imagine if your only concern was making Jesus known, even if no one ever remembered your name.

What would happen if we began to put aside our self-seeking ambitions and joyfully take the lowest place, just as Jesus did? How much more of Jesus would people see in our lives if we adopted the attitude, "I must decrease, but He must increase"?

MAKING THE EXCHANGE

If you are ready to choose self-denial over self-promotion, here are some practical ways to do just that:

1. TRADE SELF-ESTEEM FOR *Christ-Esteem*

Today's beauty and fashion industries promote a truly impossible standard for feminine beauty ("If you don't look like a swimsuit model, you aren't good enough!") and consequently many women are left feeling more insecure than ever. To combat the rampant problem of female insecurity, the self-esteem message often seems like a perfect solution. After all, if little girls can learn to love themselves regardless of whether society applauds them, they won't struggle with low self-esteem (and the poor choices that result from this attitude) as they grow older. And if women can learn to feel good about themselves regardless of their appearance or personal failures, they won't wallow in self-condemnation and bring their marriages and families down in the process.

But learning how to love and feel good about ourselves is not the solution to overcoming insecurity. Yes, it is important to understand how precious we are in God's sight—so valuable, in fact, that He gave His only Son to rescue us. We should value our lives because we are made in the image of God; we are His creation. His love for us is truly unfathomable. And as Christian women, we are daughters of the King, redeemed and made into royalty through the work of the Cross. But when we make feeling good about ourselves a focal point, we take our eyes off Christ and become wrapped up in self.

Scripture tells us that we are not to have confidence in ourselves, but in Christ only (see Phil. 3:3). In fact, Paul goes so far as to say that he counts all his personal accomplishments "as rubbish" compared to the surpassing greatness of knowing Christ (see Phil. 3:8).

Jesus does not mince words on this point: "If anyone desires to come after Me, let him deny himself, and take up his cross daily, and follow Me" (Lk. 9:23), and "He who does not take his cross and follow after Me is not worthy of Me" (Mt. 10:38).

It may seem hard to believe that self-denial, rather than self-esteem, could be the solution to insecurity. But when we let self fade into the background and become consumed with Jesus Christ, our insecurities will melt away. We no longer look to ourselves—our own merit, talent, beauty, or uniqueness—to find confidence. Instead, we learn to find our confidence in who *He* is, rather than in who *we* are.

Ian Thomas captured this principle so well when he wrote:

The Christian life can be explained only in terms of Jesus Christ, and if your life as a Christian can still be explained in terms of *you*—*your* personality, *your* willpower, *your* gift, *your* talent, *your* money, *your* courage, *your* scholarship, *your* dedication, *your* sacrifice, or *your* anything—then although you may *have* the Christian life, you are not yet living it![4]

And Charles Spurgeon echoed the same truth with his words:

If any soul has any . . . beauty, Christ has endowed that beloved soul with all its wealth and charms, for in ourselves we are deformed and defiled! . . . There is no beauty in any of us but what our Lord has worked in us.[5]

Today we are often led to believe that we all have beauty within us and that if we could only learn to love ourselves just the way we are, we would be confident and happy. But the reality is, as Spurgeon so straightforwardly put it, we do not possess any beauty or goodness of our own accord (see Pss. 14:3; 16:2; 53:3). The only beauty or merit we can ever have is Jesus Christ's. And His loveliness will only come shining through our lives when self has gotten out of the way. (Remember, we must decrease so that He might increase!)

Rather than trying to build up our self-esteem and feel good about ourselves (which doesn't produce lasting confidence anyway), we must let thoughts of self fade into the background. Remember that to "deny ourselves" according to the biblical pattern literally means to lose sight of ourselves and our own interests. We will only gain lasting security when we look *away* from ourselves and *toward* Jesus Christ. The question "who am *I*?" is not nearly as important as the question "who is *He*?"

There are two very different ways in which we can fall into the trap of focusing on ourselves instead of Christ. Sometimes, the Enemy will stroke us with pride, whispering flattering words about how special and important we are, and encouraging us to celebrate our own uniqueness and beauty. We might even go so far as to believe that when *we* are noticed and applauded, Christ will be glorified through our lives. A popular Christian book exhorts women to live to their glory, inhabit their beauty, and let "self [flash] off frame and face."[6] But this attitude produces a woman who is self-confident rather than

Christ-confident. She may have self-esteem, but she's drawing her security from *within,* instead of *from Him.* When others encounter her life, they notice her, not Jesus. She may talk a lot *about* Jesus, but her focus is on herself.

If you have a tendency to think highly of yourself, take some time to meditate upon the incredible humility of Jesus Christ (see Phil. 2:5-8). Ask God to work that same humility within you. Be willing to take a step back from any area in which you find your identity outside of Christ. For example, if publicly demonstrating your talents (performing, competing, DIY crafting and blogging, and so on) tempts you toward pride, consider taking a season away from those things until your only concern is knowing Christ and making Him known, rather than being applauded for your gifts. Ask God to give you the same heart-attitude as Jackie Pullinger, who was content to perform her acts of service for heaven's eyes alone. So it must be with us. But we cannot gain that attitude on our own. Only the grace of God can change a prideful heart into a humble one. Surrender to Him and ask Him to work this profound transformation in your soul. It is a prayer He delights to answer (see Jas. 4:6).

On the flip side, if the Enemy can't get us to take the bait of pride, he'll often hit us with accusation and discouragement. (This is the one I'm most prone to!) His goal is to turn our eyes away from Jesus Christ and onto our own shortcomings. Satan loves to see us become consumed with our own failures, placing more confidence in our own weaknesses than in the power of Christ to forgive and transform us.

Being in Christ means that we have access to the throne room of grace—not based on our merit, skill, talent, or ability to be perfect, but simply because we are clothed in His righteousness. We can meditate upon His perfection, rather than dwelling on all our own imperfections. I often turn to the Psalms for this purpose, especially the ones that focus on the majesty, glory, perfection, and faithfulness of our God, such as Psalms 29, 96, and 103.

If you tend to wallow in insecurity and accusation, take some time to meditate upon His perfection, such as by reading the Psalms just mentioned. Ask Him to turn your eyes away from your own mistakes and on to His incredible strength, power, and holiness. Remember that there is "no condemnation to those who are in Christ Jesus" (Ro. 8:1).

God desires that we would learn to esteem Jesus Christ, not ourselves. When He is in His rightful place in our lives and hearts, insecurity is replaced with a confidence that cannot be shaken, because it's in Him.

2. POINT OTHERS TO *Jesus*

When my husband and I were first getting to know each other, my dad made the observation, "Ever since Eric has been in your life, you have grown closer to Jesus Christ." I had never had a friendship with anyone, especially a young man, who continually pointed me to Jesus the way that Eric did. When we spent time around each other, I was inspired and challenged by his passion for Scripture and enthusiasm for the things of God. I remember thinking many times,

I want to know Jesus the way Eric Ludy knows Him. Often after spending time around Eric, I would end up alone in my room with a Bible open in my lap, poring over the Scriptures and seeking a deeper relationship with Christ.

Though Eric had a dynamic personality, he had an amazing way of deflecting attention away from himself and toward Jesus. It's not that the only thing he ever talked about was Jesus (though he did find a way onto that subject quite often!), but his overall attitude and focus was centered on heavenly things instead of earthly ones, and he was marked by godly humility. He did not boast about his accomplishments or show off his intelligence or witty humor. Though he was outgoing, he always found ways to encourage those around him and build others up, rather than constantly trying to take center stage. He didn't seem concerned with building up his own image, but he was passionate about showcasing the love of Christ to everyone with whom he came in contact. Even if he didn't specifically share the Gospel with his words, he continually shared the Gospel through his life and example.

Ever since that time it has been my goal to point others toward Christ when I interact with them. I have the type of personality that naturally desires approval from others. But God says, "The fear of man brings a snare" (Prov. 29:25). So instead of worrying about what people are thinking of me or trying to build up my value in their eyes, I must choose to uplift, encourage, and exhort those around me— to demonstrate the nature of Christ through my words, example, expression, and attitude. I don't always succeed at doing this; there are times when I allow insecurity or self-ishness to hinder me from showcasing the Gospel to others. But I have found that when I purposefully ask, "How can I show Jesus to this person right now?" God gives me the wisdom and grace I need in order to point others' eyes toward Him.

3. BE MINDFUL OF *Social Pitfalls*

When it comes to social interaction, women seem especially prone to things like flirting, gossip, manipulation, and the rapidly growing "selfie" trend. None of these activities, no matter how harmless they may seem at the time, will assist us in pointing others toward Jesus Christ. In fact, they will hinder our ability to do so. Let's take a closer look at each of these social pitfalls:

Flirting. Many single women assume that a little flirt-ing here and there is harmless. Many even think it's a great way to find out if a guy is interested in them. But there is no purpose for flirting other than to draw someone's atten-tion to yourself. When you flirt, you employ your feminine wiles, personality, and wit to get guys to notice and appreci-ate you. The men you are flirting with aren't thinking about Jesus; they are thinking about *you.* When you are flirting, it will not be the light of Christ in your eyes or the example of love and purity flowing from your life that attracts someone to you, but your own personality and charm.

Proverbs 7:10-27 describes a woman who is boister-ous, loud, and constantly on the prowl for men. When she finds a man she likes, she dresses seductively and uses enticing, manipulative words to allure him. The Bible says this is deadly: "Do not let your heart turn aside to her ways, do not stray into her paths; for she has cast down many wounded, and all who were slain by her were strong men. Her house is the way to hell, descending to the chambers of death" (Prov. 7:25-27).

Scripture praises women who have the quality of discretion, who possess a gentle and quiet spirit and showcase selfless love (see Titus 2:5; 1 Pet. 3:4; 1 Tim. 5:10). If you are single, one of the best ways that you can begin pointing men's eyes toward Christ instead of yourself is to forsake flirting and embrace a quiet, Christ-centered spirit instead. Remember, a Christ-built man will be drawn to you because of your undivided focus on Jesus Christ, not because of your flirting skills! (For more on this subject, please see my book *Answering the Guy Questions*.)

Gossip. We addressed the subject of gossip in the previous chapter, but it is worth mentioning again here because if you are gossiping, you are not pointing others toward Jesus Christ. And again, beware of "spiritualized gossip" that drips with sweet-sounding words that actually cast a slur upon someone else (for example, "We really need to pray for so-and-so, because . . ."). Through gossip, women often seek to build themselves up by tearing others down.

Gossip is a sin that breaks God's heart and pulls us away from Him (see Prov. 20:19; 2 Cor. 12:20). It is impossible to showcase the nature of Christ when spreading seeds of poison against someone else. If you have a weakness in this area, ask God to transform your heart and teach you how to speak words of life, rather than words of death.

Manipulation. Whether in the form of sulking and ignoring someone who's offended us, gushing flattery upon someone who might help elevate our popularity status, or dropping hints about our unique qualities to a prospective boss or future husband, manipulation diminishes our ability to reflect Jesus to those around us. Those of us who are married are often tempted to use manipulation to try to get our husbands to behave the way we want them to. Storming around the house and slamming doors might seem like the easiest way to get our husband to "wake up and smell the coffee," but the Bible says that it is "better to dwell in the wilderness, than with a contentious and angry woman" (Prov. 21:19).

In short, a manipulative woman is one who attempts to control people around her. There is nothing lovely or inspiring about manipulation. In fact, it is impossible to demonstrate the kind of Christlike love outlined in 1 Corinthians 13 ("Love is patient, love is kind. It does not envy . . .") when we are manipulating others.

Prayerfully examine your interaction with the people you regularly encounter (husband, siblings, parents, friends, coworkers, and so on). Ask God to show you any way—small or big—in which you tend to be manipulative in those relationships. For example, do you carry a chip on your shoulder toward friends, roommates, or coworkers until they apologize for stepping on your toes? Do you emotionally punish your husband when he's less than perfect? Do you pour flattery upon certain people because of your own selfish ulterior motives?

If God reveals any area of manipulation in your life, ask Him to forgive you and grant you the grace to turn and walk the other direction. Write down any specific patterns in which you desire to exchange selfish control for Christ-like love, sincerity, and gentleness. Take some time to study and even memorize 1 Corinthians 13, and ask God to weave those qualities into the fabric of your character, by His grace. A woman who is gracious, sincere, and quick to forgive is a beautiful picture of heaven.

Selfies. A "selfie" is a smartphone snapshot of yourself that you post on Facebook, Instagram, or other forms of social media. The selfie has gotten so popular among even Christian women that it can be tempting to jump on the bandwagon. Besides, not all selfies are harmful. Taking a snapshot of yourself and sending it to a family member with the message "I love you" or "I'm thinking of you" can be a blessing to them. However, if you make a habit out of taking self-portrait photos and posting them publicly, you can easily fall into the trap of drawing attention to yourself instead of to Jesus.

Take a look at this excerpt from an online article on webtrends.com, examining the sociological reasons why people take selfies:

To get attention from as many people as possible:
People like to get noticed on social media, and all of
those "likes" and comments from friends are a quick
and easy way to fish for compliments and boost
one's own ego. **To get a self-esteem boost:** . . . Many
[people] might upload selfies to deal with their own
self-consciousness. **To show off:** It's human nature
to want to show off your own great achievements.
When you feel good about yourself (or look good),
it's far too easy to reach for your phone and
document it all through one (or several) selfies.[7]

That article says it more straightforwardly than most
Christians would dare to! Think about that list for a moment.
Do any of those motives line up with God's desire for us to
decrease so that He might increase in our lives?

A godly single man recently offered a great perspective
on selfies in an online article for my ministry, setapartgirl™.
He wrote:

Taking pictures of yourself and posting "selfies" all
day long is the in thing to do, but honestly it is not
very inspiring to a [godly young man]. Don't get me
wrong, not all "selfies" are bad. But the principle
here is that to be a great sister in Christ, focus on
pointing others to Jesus instead of yourself. I admire
my sisters and see a tremendous beauty within them
when they are outwardly focused and pointing

people to Christ. Inversely, there is a repugnance within my soul when I see girls preoccupied with themselves even when they may be outwardly attractive. . . . Selflessness will be a great blessing to your brothers in Christ.[8]

Scripture is filled with exhortations to exchange self-promotion for self-denial. Here are just a few samplings:

[Love] does not seek its own.
(1 COR. 13:5)

For whoever exalts himself will be humbled, and he who humbles himself will be exalted.
(LK. 14:11)

God opposes the proud, but gives grace to the humble.
(JAS. 4:6, ESV)

In lowliness of mind let each esteem others better than himself.
(PHIL. 2:3)

Do not think of yourself more highly than you ought, but rather think of yourself with sober judgment.
(RO. 12:3, NIV)

> Let no one seek his own, but each one the other's well-being.
>
> (1 COR. 10:24)

And yet, there is perhaps nothing more challenging to our flesh (that selfish, sinful part of us that craves control) than to lay down our pride and willingly "take the lowest place" as Jesus did. When we choose humility, we are choosing the very attitude of Christ, as it says in Philippians 2:5. And there is no better way for the beauty of heaven to come cascading through our lives than to get out of the way so that He can be clearly seen.

A set-apart woman does not get between God and His glory. What amazing possibilities await when we decrease, that He might increase! (To go deeper into this topic, I recommend the message "Ten Shekels and a Shirt" by Paris Reidhead, available for free download at www.sermonindex.net.)

LET'S TALK ABOUT IT

Group Study and Discussion

1. **READ MATTHEW 16:24.** What is the difference between self-promotion and self-denial? When we chose godly humility over self-promotion, what do our lives look like?

2. **READ PHILIPPIANS 2:7 AND JAMES 4:6.** What kind of humility has Christ called us to? When we are humble, how does it affect our relationship with Christ?

TAKE IT DEEPER

Personal Study and Reflection

READ: JOHN 3:30

REFLECT: Do I draw others' attention toward myself, or toward Christ? Am I willing to get out of the way so that He can be more clearly seen through me? What practical changes must I make in my life in order to do this?

READ: PHILIPPIANS 2:3-4

REFLECT: Do I have selfish ambition or conceit in my life? Am I ready to repent of these sins and ask God to remake me into a reflection of godly humility? (If yes, take some time to lay down your pride and selfish ambition and embrace a life of humility by His grace.)

CHAPTER SEVEN

An Undivided Heart

Exchanging Idolatry for Faithfulness

"She . . . went after her lovers; but Me she forgot," says the LORD.

HOSEA 2:13

No one can serve two masters; for either he will hate the one and love the other, or else he will be loyal to the one and despise the other.

MATTHEW 6:24

What kind of habitation pleases God? What must our natures be like before He can feel at home within us? He asks nothing but a pure heart and a single mind.

A. W. TOZER, *That Incredible Christian*

Father, let me . . . loose my clutch on everything temporal. My life, my reputation, my possessions, Lord, let me loose the tension of the grasping hand. . . . Open my hand to receive the nail of Calvary, as Christ's was opened . . . He thought Heaven, yea, equality with God, not a thing to be clutched at. So let me release my grasp.

JIM ELLIOT, *Shadow of the Almighty*

WHEN I WAS GROWING UP, my mom was considered by most standards to be a health nut. My friends' lunch boxes contained white bread sandwiches, greasy potato chips, and Little Debbie cupcakes, while mine was filled with whole wheat bread, carrot sticks, and sugar-free granola bars. In our house, eating "sugar cereal" like Froot Loops or Cap'n Crunch for breakfast was akin to cheating on our homework assignments. Kids who ate that kind of "garbage," we were told, ended up in detention and remedial reading classes, not to mention making frequent and painful trips to the dentist's office to have their many cavities filled.

So to my great consternation, we ate Cream of Wheat or oatmeal nearly every morning, a habit which my mom assured us would lead to good grades, healthy teeth, and respectable behavior at school. I constantly complained about having to eat healthy food, and balked at every green item my mom put on my plate, be it peas, lettuce, or spinach. To say that I was a picky eater was putting it mildly.

By the time I was thirteen, my mom was sick and tired of fighting battles with me over food. In a moment of frustration she declared, "Okay, Leslie, from now on I am not going to force healthy food on you. You decide what you eat. But you reap the consequences."

At that age I wasn't thinking too much about consequences; I was simply overjoyed that my mom had given me the freedom I had been dreaming of for years. Finally I was allowed to buy my own box of Lucky Charms (I had to use babysitting money because my mom wouldn't touch the stuff) and eat as much as I wanted! I could splurge on a huge bag of M&M's and keep them in my locker at school! Most of my friends had grown up eating junk food, but I had been deprived. Now, I needed to make up for lost time. And that is exactly what I did. I don't think I so much as touched a vegetable for about two years. I splurged on candy and ice cream whenever the mood struck. I ate pizza for lunch almost every day. My health suffered, but I was so addicted to the pleasure of eating whatever I craved that I didn't care.

When God got ahold of my life several years later, He began to gently put His finger on many areas that needed to change. My diet was one of them. I read in Philippians 3:19 that sinful people made their stomach their god, blindly serving the cravings of their physical bodies. And I realized this was exactly what I had been doing.

So, by the grace of God, I purposed to honor Him in my eating habits instead of indulging my selfish whims and desires. As I developed greater discipline in my eating habits, my health and energy level improved dramatically. Both physically and spiritually, I saw enormous benefits from removing my addiction to junk food and choosing not to be enslaved to my personal appetites and cravings. But what started out as a step of obedience to God soon grew into something very different.

The more I studied nutrition, the more intrigued I became. Reading through health books and websites,

I learned how toxic the standard American diet was, to the point where I became horrified at the thought of ever eating at McDonald's again. I discovered the incredible benefits of vegetables, fruits, and whole grains, and began to go to extremes to get these nutrients into my diet, drinking raw vegetable juice concoctions several times a day, eating only salads for lunch and dinner, and forcing myself to drink a large mixture of Barleygreen powder every night before bed.

The more I read the latest news in nutritional research, the more paranoid I became about what I ate. I had never worried about serious diseases, but now I found myself believing that if I didn't eat exactly the right way, my body would fall apart. It was all up to me to protect my health. After all, didn't God want me to take care of the body He had given me?

Time that should have been spent in God's presence was now spent studying health trends. Hours that should have been given to serving others were now spent shopping at the health food store, preparing healthy meals, and juicing raw fruits and veggies multiple times a day. I couldn't travel without bringing an entire suitcase filled with my healthy food. At parties or dinner engagements, I couldn't eat what was served because I knew how bad it was for me and I was convinced it would make me sick. My identity became wrapped up in my healthy lifestyle instead of in my relationship with Christ. I found myself subtly looking down on other people who didn't place as high a value on healthy eating as I did.

Instead of simply being all about Jesus, I had become all about healthy eating, with Jesus somewhere in the background.

Once again, God convicted me. Healthy eating was fine and good, as long as it didn't become the center of my life. Before I'd been addicted to self-indulgence, but now I had become addicted to self-protection. Both attitudes stood in the way of my ability to seek Jesus Christ with an undivided heart. As I yielded to the conviction of God's Spirit and studied His Word on these points, I came to the realization that food had become a form of idolatry in my life, dividing my heart and stealing my focus away from Christ.

IDENTIFYING OUR IDOLS

I used to believe that all idols were golden statues in ornate temples and that as long as I wasn't bowing to them, I didn't have idolatry in my life. But as I've studied Scripture and grown deeper in my relationship with Christ, I've realized that an idol is anything or anyone that takes a higher position than Jesus Christ in my heart and life, anything that claims more of my devotion and affection than Him. Our God is a jealous God, and He wants our entire heart, not just part of it (see Ex. 20:5). He says, "I am the LORD; that is my name! I will not yield my glory to another or my praise to idols" (Is. 42:8, NIV) and, "Worship the LORD your God and serve him only" (Lk. 4:8, NIV).

The psalmist prayed, "Give me an undivided heart, that I may fear your name" (Ps. 86:11, NIV). Idolatry divides our hearts from Christ. Matthew 6:24 says, "No one can serve two masters; for either he will hate the one and love the other, or else he will be loyal to the one and despise the other." When we have idolatry in our lives, we may say (or even believe) that Jesus Christ has our whole heart, but in reality we place our hopes and affections in pursuits outside of Him (health, money, romance, and so on). Scripture is clear: When we become slaves to our appetites, our health or financial goals, our romantic pursuits, our popularity, our comforts, or anything else, we *cannot* be the servants of Christ.

How often do we stand in a worship service and sing songs like "You Are My All in All" while our minds are preoccupied with thoughts of a relationship or a career opportunity? How often is our identity far more wrapped up in our popularity, achievements, or possessions than in the simple, glorious reality that we are daughters of the King? How often do we think, *If I could only* [get married, make more money, lose weight, have more friends, do something exciting, and so on], *THEN I would be happy, and I would make Jesus my number one focus*? We ask God to give us the desires of our hearts, all the while forgetting that *He* should always be the chief desire of our hearts.

Idolatry sneaks into our lives in a variety of ways. When the gaze of our soul does not remain fixed upon Jesus Christ, good desires (such as taking care of our bodies, waiting for a godly spouse, or cultivating friendships) can morph into unhealthy preoccupations before we realize what has happened. A simple intention to eat right can turn into a fixation with health, a God-given longing for marriage can become an obsessive need to find a guy, and a healthy desire for friendship can become an addiction to approval and popularity. Often, the biggest threats to seeking Christ with an undivided heart are not overtly sinful things, but good and God-given desires that subtly start to claim too much of our focus and affection.

So how can you know when something has become an idol in your life? Here are some of the most common warning signs:

1. *You can't imagine giving it up.* You think: *If I don't eat health food, I'll surely die an early death;* or, *If I can't listen to my favorite music every day, I'll be miserable and depressed;* or, *If I don't get married, life won't be worth living.*

2. *You spend more time and energy on that area than you do on your relationship with Christ.* For instance, maybe you spend eight hours each week on movies or social media, but only ten minutes in prayer or in studying God's Word. Or maybe you invest the majority of your time and energy into a relationship (or the pursuit of one) and have little time left over to seek Christ or share Him with others. As much as we don't like to admit it, the areas that claim the majority of our spare time are those that have the biggest hold upon our hearts.

3. *You find more delight and happiness in that area of your life than you do in your relationship with Christ.*

It's not wrong if earthly things bring us a certain level of comfort or happiness. But Jesus must always remain our source of deepest satisfaction. A great way to determine whether you are finding your fulfillment in Christ is to ask yourself the question, "If this area of my life was suddenly stripped away from me, would Jesus be enough?"

PUTTING JESUS FIRST

Remember the pastor who was in solitary confinement for a year? Every comfort was taken away from him, but he still had everything he needed in Christ alone. He was not attempting to serve Christ while also serving his appetite, cravings, ambitions, and whims. His heart was fixed upon only one thing: his relationship with his precious King. He triumphed through his sufferings because he had an undivided heart.

Sabina Wurmbrand was a young pastor's wife during the Communist invasion of Romania in 1944. She had a happy, secure life with her husband and young son. But one day, she was forced to make a choice of what was more important to her—her marriage and family, or Jesus Christ. As she and her husband, Richard, sat in a meeting led by Communists, they listened as many pastors and Christians blasphemed the name of Christ out of fear of the government officials. Her heart broke as Christ's name was being dishonored. She said to her husband, "Will you not wash this shame from the face of Christ?" He told her, "If I do, you will no longer have a husband." She boldly replied, "I don't need a coward for a husband." Those bold words gave Richard the strength he needed to stand up and speak the Truth, though he knew it might cost him his life. Sabina loved her husband. But she was willing to sacrifice the secure life she shared with him, because she loved Jesus more.[1]

Sabina's decision to encourage her husband to speak up that day resulted in his imprisonment and torture for ten long years. She herself was imprisoned for four years in horrific and abusive conditions. She and her family suffered years of poverty and incredible persecution because they were willing to put Jesus higher than their own comforts and security.[2]

Countless Christians through the ages, and today in persecuted countries around the world, have made astounding personal sacrifices, even giving up their very lives, in order to put Jesus first. If these men and women are willing to give up everything in order to serve only one Master, Jesus Christ, can we not do the same? If we are not cultivating an undivided heart toward Christ *right now* in areas such as food, money, and romance, how can we expect to keep our gaze fixed upon Him when greater trials and sufferings come?

MAKING THE EXCHANGE

Becoming a set-apart woman means being willing to forsake any pursuit or affection that hinders your ability to be fully consecrated to Jesus Christ. If you are ready to remove idolatry from your life and gain an undivided heart toward Christ, here are some areas to prayerfully examine:

1. SELF-*Indulgence*

As Americans, we live in one of the wealthiest, most self-indulgent nations in history. Few people on earth have ever had so many food choices, so many leisure opportunities, and so many creative ways to indulge our physical cravings. Feel like a hot fudge sundae? Just drive down the road to your local Dairy Queen! In the mood for a juicy steak? All you need to do is find the nearest steak house! Want to get pampered? There's a spa around the corner! Longing for a luxurious beach getaway? Just hop online and book your tickets! Need a frothy caffeine fix? Starbucks coffee shops are everywhere! Not only is it easy to indulge ourselves, we're encouraged by advertisers to do so: "Go ahead, treat yourself. You deserve it."

One of the best ways to be considered hip and trendy these days is to call yourself a foodie and become a connoisseur of great food. Foodies, by definition, are people who not only enjoy good food, but build their lives around food. It's easy to jump on this bandwagon because everyone else is doing it—and besides, how could enjoying good food possibly cause harm to our spiritual lives?

The danger is not in enjoying food or other comforts, but in letting our physical cravings lead and control us. The Bible warns against making our appetite our god (see Phil. 3:19). And Paul said, "I discipline my body and bring it into subjection, lest, when I have preached to others, I myself should become disqualified" (1 Cor. 9:27). Most of us in the modern Western world don't think twice about self-indulgence because it is the norm. But God asks us to put a harness on our physical cravings and desires, so that self-indulgence does not become an idol in our lives. When we become slaves to our appetites, we cannot be the devoted servants of Christ that we are called to be.

Remember, it's not wrong to find pleasure in the comforts of this life, such as good food, physical rest, or fun, refreshing activities. (Also, preparing delicious meals as a means of giving can be a wonderful way to bless others with Christ's love.) But when we can't live without our favorite cereal or our daily Starbucks fix, when we indulge our every craving without restraint, and when we put personal comforts above our ability to seek Christ or serve others, that's when we know that we've allowed the idolatry of self-indulgence to creep in.

Ask God to show you any areas of your life, food or otherwise, in which you are controlled by your appetite, rather than by His Spirit. Write down practical steps He brings to mind for making a shift of pattern in these areas. Remember not to lean upon willpower in an attempt to bring your physical cravings under control. Rather, ask God for His supernatural enabling power to do what is impossible in your own strength. As you yield your heart, mind, and body to Him, He will grant you the grace for every step of obedience He calls you to. (For more on this subject, I encourage you to listen to the message "Foodies," available for free download at www.ellerslie.com.)

2. WORLDLY *Entertainment*

Leonard Ravenhill observed, "American Christians have settled for a counterfeit peace and a counterfeit joy, and their names are Entertainment and Professional Sports."[3] I agree. Many people, including Christians, build their lives around entertainment. As we discussed in chapter 4, movies, T.V., music, magazines, novels, social media, and professional sports consume the vast majority of our free time. But worldly entertainment not only distracts us from Christ and keeps us focused on the temporal instead of the eternal, for many it has also become a form of idolatry. When we participate in the ungodly preoccupations of the culture, it is impossible for us to seek Jesus Christ with an undivided heart. God makes it clear that we cannot love both Him *and* the things of this world:

> Adulterers and adulteresses! Do you not know that friendship with the world is enmity with God? Whoever therefore wants to be a friend of the world makes himself an enemy of God.
>
> (JAS. 4:4)

> Do not love the world or the things in the world. If anyone loves the world, the love of the Father is not in him. For all that is in the world—the lust of the

flesh, the lust of the eyes, and the pride of life—is
not of the Father but is of the world.
(1 JN. 2:15-16)

Spend five minutes watching a modern T.V. show or
a series of commercials and you realize that worldly entertainment is built upon the Gospel-choking pitfalls warned
against in Scripture: "the lust of the flesh" ("Here's a new way
to indulge your physical cravings!"); "the lust of the eyes"
("Look at this beautiful new car; don't you want one?"); and
"the pride of life" ("It's all about *me*!").

Yet we constantly justify our preoccupation with these
activities, thinking that we are somehow immune to God's
warnings against them, because we are mature enough to
separate the garbage from the good. We come up with wise-
sounding excuses such as, "God knows I don't agree with
everything in this movie. I'll just ignore the immorality and
enjoy the amazing artistry of this film," or, "I have to watch
T.V. or else I won't be in tune with where the culture is at," or,
"My friends and family members all build their lives around
these activities, and participating with them is the only way
I can show my love to them."

When we reason this way, we end up corrupting our
hearts and minds by idolizing our "right" to be entertained
and catered to by pop culture. We often start to idolize the
icons of the world: professional athletes, movie and T.V. stars,
musicians, and so on. A lot of us would rather spend an hour
backstage with our favorite musician than an hour sitting at

the feet of Jesus. We buy into the larger-than-life image that celebrities exude, and think of them as "gods" deserving of our devoted affection and special attention. Sadly, we often care far more about their opinions than we do about God's.

When it comes to worldly entertainment, we must be extra guarded against idolatry, both toward becoming addicted to pop culture and in becoming enamored with worldly icons and celebrities. We must learn to view the shallow, ungodly attractions of this world the way God sees them: as worthless, meaningless, and empty. No matter how much glitz and artistry Hollywood may use to dazzle our senses and draw our attention, if it does not glorify God and draw us closer to Him, it is dangerous to our souls. May our attitude toward pop culture attractions echo that of the psalmist when he said, "Turn away my eyes from looking at worthless things, and revive me in Your way" (Ps. 119:37).

It might seem that living a life that is not built around worldly entertainment would be dull, or that not watching T.V. regularly would cause you to become out of touch with the culture and unable to impact the world for Christ. But I have discovered that the opposite is true. Once I removed this idol, I suddenly had time to pursue Christ with all my heart; I became free to live the exciting adventure He had planned for me each day. And once I stopped assaulting my spiritual senses with the ungodly messages of the culture, I became much more in tune with the voice of God's Spirit and far more equipped to make a lasting impact on the world around me.

Prayerfully consider any areas of entertainment that have become unhealthy addictions in your life—music, movies, T.V. shows, sports, novels, and so on. Ask God to show you what activities need to be removed from your life and what activities might need to be put in their proper place (for instance, watching an edifying movie every once in a while, instead of watching movies two or three nights a week). Ask Him for the grace to change your habits in order to be consecrated to Him in this area of your life. Make these decisions out of love for Him, not out of legalism, obligation, or a self-righteous "statement" toward other Christians in your life who might not share your same standards.

Remember, this life is but a breath (see Ps. 39:5). In light of eternity, what will matter more . . . whether you saw all the latest Hollywood productions, or whether you kept your eyes fixed solely upon the unmatched glory, loveliness, and majesty of Jesus?

3. HEALTH, FITNESS, AND *Beauty*

I have already shared how healthy eating became a form of idolatry earlier in my life. It's something I must still be guarded about, even all these years later. Living in Colorado (recently voted one of the most health-conscious states in the country), I'm surrounded by the health and fitness craze. Dedicated joggers and disciplined road bikers can be seen on nearly every street. Gluten-free bread and organic produce can be found in almost every store. (I've even noticed vegetarian convenience food in several gas stations.) Vegan restaurants are common. And health food stores are as easily accessed as regular grocery stores. Everywhere I go, it seems I'm bombarded with messages like, "This revolutionary health breakthrough will change your life!" or "This amazing new diet will keep you young into your nineties!" Though I enjoy the benefits of eating healthy food, I must remind myself that Jesus, not a specific health program, is my true source of life and strength.

Even though Scripture makes it clear that "life is more than food" (Lk. 12:23), it's all too easy to believe otherwise. If we don't fall into the trap of self-indulgence in our eating habits, we often lean too far in the other direction—exalting health food and fitness and placing our hope in our diet and exercise habits instead of in Jesus Christ.

Living a healthful lifestyle can be a wonderful way to serve our families, bring discipline into our lives, and keep our bodies strong for the things God has called us to. But it can also become a form of idolatry if we build our lives around health instead of around Christ.

Many Christian women take great pride in cooking healthy meals for their families and treating their kids' ailments with natural remedies and herbal supplements. But what starts out as a tool with which we can care for our families can easily become an unhealthy preoccupation if we aren't careful. We shouldn't find our identity in being a health food enthusiast. Our identity should be found in Christ alone.

What if America was hit by a devastating war or extreme persecution broke out against Christians, as it has in so many other places around the world? Our ability to run to Whole Foods each week and buy all organic produce or grass-fed meats might be hampered. Do we trust that God would still sustain us and give us the strength to live out our callings, even if we were to find ourselves in a situation where we can't take vitamins or make green smoothies every day? So that leads us to an important question: How can we be good stewards of our health without letting it become a primary focus in our lives?

We must examine our motives for why we are exercising and eating right. Is it because we are trying to self-preserve and self-protect, or because we desire to be strong and ready to live for Jesus Christ? The world idolizes health and fitness for selfish reasons; they want to maintain a "sexy lean body" and look young their whole lives. But a Christian woman takes care of her body as an outflow of her love for Jesus Christ. She shows respect for the body God has given her, not so that she can maintain a certain image or ideal weight, but so that she will be strong and able to give to and serve those around her (see Prov. 31:17), or even to suffer well for Jesus Christ if He calls her to.

Rachel Jankovic in her book, *Loving the Little Years*, expressed this principle well:

> Our bodies are tools, not treasures. You should not spend your days trying to preserve your body in its eighteen-year-old form. Let it be used [for God's purposes]. . . . We are not to treat our bodies like museum pieces. They were not given to us to

preserve, they were given to us to use. So use [your body] cheerfully, and maintain it cheerfully.[4]

Esther Ahn Kim was a courageous young woman who stood boldly for Christ in Korea during the Japanese invasion in 1939. When she made the decision not to bow at a Japanese shrine, she knew it was only a matter of time before she was caught and imprisoned for the stand that she had taken for Christ. But instead of cowering in fear and worry about what her future held, she decided to prepare her heart and her body to suffer for Christ. Esther decided to train for prison life, just as an athlete might train for competitive sports. She counted it a great honor to suffer for Christ, but she also knew she was weak and unready for all that lay ahead. She spent time fasting, training her body to go for long periods of time without food.

Esther also began sleeping on the floor, learning to live in a state of poverty, eating rotten produce, and going without all the comforts she had grown up with, so that she would be prepared for the harsh conditions of prison. Months of faithful, diligent preparation—fasting, memorizing Scripture, tirelessly praying, and training to endure harsh conditions—transformed Esther from a frail young woman to a bold and confident ambassador for Christ. Instead of fearing torture, she now faced it boldly in the power and grace of God.[5] What an amazing difference from the self-focused, self-preserving approach to discipline, fitness, and health that we see all around us today!

If health and exercise have claimed too much of your

focus (or if they have been a focus for the wrong reasons), prayerfully consider what steps God might be asking you to take in order to change this pattern. Start by asking God to purify your motives for taking care of your body and the health of your family, to give you a heart that longs to honor Him rather than simply to preserve your own image.

Allow Him to gently show you any ways in which you have been leaning on your healthy habits instead of on Him to find strength and peace. And take the steps of obedience He asks you to take, whether it means relaxing more about the food you eat or spending less time obsessing over which vitamins you should be taking, and more time building the kingdom of God. He will be faithful to build you strong for what He has called you to when you make faith, not food, the focus of your life.

4. MARRIAGE AND *Family*

One of the most baffling statements Jesus ever made was, "If anyone comes to Me and does not hate his father and mother, wife and children, brothers and sisters, yes, and his own life also, he cannot be My disciple" (Lk. 14:26). The same Bible that tells us to honor our father and mother and respect our husband and love our children seems to be saying that we cannot follow Christ unless we "hate" our own family members. So what is this all about?

Once again, God is reminding us not to place *anything* above Jesus Christ, even the good and perfect gifts that He gives us, such as our families. Though it is obvious from the rest of Scripture that He does not desire us to hate our family members in a spiteful, sinful way, it is also clear that we are never to put a higher priority on marriage and family than we do on Jesus Christ.

This form of idolatry often begins before we've even met our future husband. When we are single, we often believe that we will only be happy once we meet Prince Charming and settle down in a cute house with a white picket fence. (I know I certainly struggled with this mind-set during my single years!) I can't count the number of single women I've met who build their entire lives, thoughts, and emotions around the pursuit of a guy, instead of the pursuit of Jesus Christ. They think that once they find a husband, they'll discover the inner peace and fulfillment they long for, overlooking the fact that Jesus Christ alone can meet the deepest desires of their hearts.

During our single years, it's tempting to both idolize *and* idealize our marriage hopes and dreams. But this is a dangerous mind-set because it keeps us from finding the perfect satisfaction in Jesus Christ that He intends for us to have. And if we expect marriage to solve the deepest needs within our soul, we'll only be placing unhealthy, unrealistic expectations upon our future husband and harming our marriage in the process.

Remember, when we are in relationship with Christ, we have everything we need for happiness right now, whether we are married or single. As Corrie ten Boom wrote, "Marriage is not the answer to unhappiness. Happiness can only be found in a balanced relationship with the Lord Jesus. . . . You can be happy with or without a husband—secure in Jesus alone."[6]

Of course, God puts a high value on marriage. It was, after all, His idea in the first place. The majority of us are called to be married. And there is certainly nothing wrong with desiring to be married, preparing for marriage, or taking steps toward a romantic relationship with someone as God leads. The problem comes when we place our marriage dreams on a pedestal, putting contentment on hold until that season of life finally comes.

Or, if we are married already, it's often tempting to cling tighter to our husbands and children than we do to Jesus Christ. God calls us to love our husbands and children (see Titus 2:4), but He calls us to love Jesus Christ *even more* (see Lk. 14:26). If we ever must make a choice between God or family, we must choose the same path that Sabina Wurmbrand did. Our security and identity must come first and foremost from Jesus Christ rather than from our marriage and family.

Women throughout history—and in persecuted countries around the world—have willingly risked their families for the sake of the Gospel. Elisabeth Elliot risked her life to live with the Auca Indians in order to reach them with the hope of Christ—even after they killed her husband and several other missionaries. Sabina Wurmbrand allowed her husband to be imprisoned for ten years in order to protect the glory of Christ's name. Corrie ten Boom and her family put one another at risk in order to protect Jews during the Holocaust, and many of them died in the process. What an amazing testimony our lives can be to this world when the glory of Jesus Christ matters far more to us even than our own life or personal comfort and security!

If marriage and family (or the hope of marriage and family) has claimed more of your affection and focus than Jesus Christ, ask God to change your heart. Freshly surrender this area of your life to Him, and remember where the deepest source of fulfillment is truly found: in Him! Meditate upon the amazing reality of all that He is. Here is just a brief sampling from Scripture of what Jesus is meant to be in our lives:

My Portion // PS. 142:5

My Maker, my Husband // IS. 54:5

My Well-Beloved // S. OF S. 1:13, KJV

My Savior // 2 PET. 3:18

My Hope // 1 TIM. 1:1

My Brother // MK. 3:35

My Helper // HEB. 13:6

My Physician // JER. 8:22

My Healer // LK. 9:11

My Refiner and my Purifier // MAL. 3:3

My Lord and Master // JN. 13:13, KJV

My Servant // LK. 12:37

My Example // JN. 13:15

My Teacher // JN. 3:2

My Shepherd // PS. 23:1

My Keeper // JN. 17:12

My Feeder // EZK. 34:23

My Leader // IS. 40:11

My Restorer // PS. 23:3

My Resting Place // JER. 50:6

My Meat and my Drink // JN. 6:55, KJV

My Passover // 1 COR. 5:7

My Peace // EPH. 2:14

My Wisdom, my Righteousness, my Sanctification, my Redemption // 1 COR. 1:30

My All in All // EPH. 1:23

Wow. Talk about the ultimate Bridegroom! As I said in my book *Sacred Singleness:*

> Such a Prince is more perfect than any fairy-tale hero that ever existed. And He invites us to have a daily romance with Him! He delights to become all of those things to us on a daily basis! And if we are in such intimate fellowship with our Lord that He fills us all in all and becomes everything in that list above, then we certainly will not try to satisfy the longings of our heart some other way![7]

5. PERSONAL *Convictions*

Personal convictions are important and necessary in every Christian's life. As the saying goes, "If you don't stand for anything, you'll fall for everything." It's vital to know what we believe and to let our lifestyle choices flow from those beliefs. I have adopted many personal convictions that have come from reading Scripture and responding to the work of God's Spirit within my soul. But as healthy as personal convictions can be, they must always be an outflow of our love for Jesus Christ, not what we find our hope and identity in. When personal convictions are placed above Christ, they make us susceptible to self-righteousness and spiritual pride.

Have you ever seen someone who was known more for her personal convictions than for her love for Jesus Christ? I remember attending a large homeschool conference just before I was married. Everywhere I looked, I saw women in long, homespun dresses, with a trail of kids in tow. Some of these women were joyful and outward focused, but the majority wore somber expressions and only seemed to acknowledge those who behaved and dressed the same way they did. In the restrooms and hallways, I heard several derogatory comments toward public-school families and toward those who didn't share their same convictions about family size and clothing choices.

While I saw nothing wrong with their convictions about homeschooling, having a lot of children, or dressing a certain way, I also realized that many of these women had begun to idolize their lifestyle choices above Jesus Christ. I couldn't help wondering how a non-Christian would respond to the Gospel if he or she encountered these women. Would a non-Christian notice the nature of Jesus shining through their lives and examples? Or would he or she only see prideful personal convictions being paraded about?

When others think of you, do they think more about your personal opinions and lifestyle choices than they do about Christ? If so, that's a sign that you might be placing too high a priority on your own convictions and opinions. Of course, that is not to say that people can't be impacted for Christ by seeing you living out your convictions. But people are far more likely to be drawn to the Gospel when they sense the attitude and nature of Jesus Christ exuding from you, rather than just noticing that your kids sit still in church or that you always wear long skirts instead of pants.

If you choose to homeschool, wear only skirts and dresses,

train your children to behave a certain way in church, sing hymns instead of choruses, choose courtship over dating, or anything else along these lines, make sure those decisions flow out of your personal relationship with Jesus Christ and are a means of showing love and honor to Him. Personal convictions should never become a means of righteousness in themselves. And again, they should never become a spiritual statement to the world around you, a way of trying to demonstrate that you are more godly than someone else. People should primarily see you as a Christian, not as a homeschooler or courtship advocate. If you find more satisfaction in the fact that you are a homeschooler, a conservative thinker, or a modest dresser—or in some other conviction—than you do in the simple, amazing, astounding fact that you are a daughter of the King, then your convictions have most certainly become an idol in your life.

That doesn't mean that homeschooling or dressing in a certain style is wrong. (I love homeschooling my children, and I am passionate about teaching young women how to dress modestly for Christ.) Your choices in those areas may be steps of obedience to God. Just be sure that you don't exalt your lifestyle choices above the Source of true life.

If you are ever imprisoned for your faith in Christ, it will certainly not be your example of homeschooling, wearing long skirts, or teaching your kids to sit still in church that will impact the prison guards and other inmates for the Gospel. Rather, it will be your hope, your faith, your gentleness, your courage, and most importantly, your love.

As it says in 1 Corinthians 13, every other demonstration of our Christianity is meaningless without this all-important foundation.

How can you tell whether a conviction has become an idol in your life?

First, evaluate your beliefs about where your righteousness and justification comes from. Do you believe that you are accepted by God because of your personal lifestyle preferences, or simply because you are "*in* Christ Jesus" (see Ro. 8:1)? If you are looking for spiritual security in anything outside of Him, you are not walking in the reality of the Gospel. Take some time to become rooted in what it means to be clothed in His righteousness and not your own. (To explore this subject further, I encourage you to listen to the message "The Poison of Political Correctness," available for free download at www.ellerslie.com.)

Second, ask yourself where your identity is coming from. As I said earlier, if you are more known for specific lifestyle choices than you are for your example of Christ, it's likely you need to readjust your priorities. That doesn't mean you should throw all your convictions out the window and go to the opposite extreme in any area of your life. But it does mean you need to shift your focus. Ask God for the grace to center your life upon Him, to make Jesus Christ and Him crucified your true North Star. And whenever you start to veer away from that true North, ask Him to gently pull your gaze back to where it belongs.

Finally, ask God to give you His heart toward Christians

who don't share your same convictions. Yes, certain foundational principles of Christianity are truly nonnegotiable. And we must be willing to divide and separate over those points, or even to die to preserve them if necessary, as Christians have done throughout the ages. But many other areas of life are not a central part of the Gospel, though we often try to make them so. If you are convinced that no one can be a Christian unless they make the same choices you do, then you need to gain a better understanding of the Gospel of Jesus Christ. Take some time to focus on the glorious, life-changing reality of the Cross and the transforming power of the Gospel. Let God build your convictions upon the things that truly matter in light of eternity, and allow the peripheral issues to be merely icing on the cake. (Note: To explore this message further, I encourage you to listen to "The Gospel Solae," available for free download at www.ellerslie.com.)

6. MONEY AND MATERIAL *Things*

Jesus said it clearly: "You cannot serve God and money" (Mt. 6:24, ESV). Even in a challenged economy, America is one of the richest countries in the world (and in all of history, for that matter!). Living in a culture where it is so easy to get what we want (be it an iPhone, a new outfit, or a new car), we often believe it is our right to have a comfortable lifestyle, purchase our dream house, drive expensive cars, and build our lives around the pursuit of "more." While there is nothing innately wrong with money or possessions, we should never build our lives around the things we have or find our identity in them (see Lk. 12:15). We should never choose the pursuit of money over the pursuit of Jesus Christ. If He blesses us with homes, cars, clothes, and other possessions, we must remember that they are not to be hoarded, but used to bless and help others. And we must always be willing to give them up at a moment's notice if He asks for them.

A rich young man once asked Jesus what he should do to inherit eternal life. The man had lived an upright, moral life and followed God's commandments faithfully from his childhood. But Jesus looked into the man's soul and saw the one thing that was standing in the way of his salvation, the idolatry of money. He told the man, "Sell all that you have and distribute to the poor, and you will have treasure in heaven; and come, follow Me" (Lk. 18:22). But the man became sad at these words. He couldn't imagine giving up his wealth. The money itself wasn't the problem; it was that his money held his heart. Even looking directly into the face of Jesus and hearing a personal invitation to follow Him, he could not let his money go.

When Jesus saw the man's response, He said, "It is easier for a camel to go through the eye of a needle than for a rich man to enter the kingdom of God" (Lk. 18:25). When we cling to money and material things, idolatry holds our souls in a vice-like grip. We can't imagine giving up the things we have, or letting go of our financial dreams and goals. And even in the face of the most amazing opportunity we will ever receive ("Sell everything and come, follow Me!"), our legs are cemented to the ground. We cannot go with Jesus, because we are imprisoned and enslaved by our possessions.

If you believe that financial security will bring you peace and happiness, not only are you making money an idol in your life but you are setting your hope upon an illusion. Proverbs 23:4-5 says, "Do not overwork to be rich; because of your own understanding, cease! Will you set your eyes on that which is not? For riches certainly make themselves wings; they fly away like an eagle toward heaven."

This world convinces us that money is important and worth focusing on. But as daughters of the King, our treasure is to be in heaven, not on this earth. Money should merely be a tool through which we can carry out God's purposes on this earth. Nothing more. It should not matter to us whether we have a lot or a little. It should only matter that we have Jesus Christ. Because if we have Him, we have everything. As Paul said, "I have learned the secret of being content in any and every situation, whether well fed or hungry, whether living in plenty or in want. I can do all this through him who gives me strength" (Phil. 4:12-13, NIV).

C. T. Studd was a wealthy English cricket player in the late 1800s when he radically gave his life to Christ. He had inherited a fortune on the day he turned twenty-five. Rather than hoard the money or attempt to use it for his own dreams and pursuits, he chose to give it all away, to invest every last dime into the kingdom of heaven. Some said this was a foolish, irresponsible act, but as C. T. studied the Scriptures, the resounding message of laying up treasures in heaven rather than on earth echoed through his soul (see Mt. 6:19-20). In C. T. Studd's biography, the author writes:

> This was no fool's plunge on his part. It was his public testimony before God and man that he believed God's Word to be the surest thing on earth, and that the hundredfold interest which God promised in this life, not to speak of the next, is an actual reality for those who believe it and act upon it.[8]

C. T.'s money went to aid Hudson Taylor's China Inland Mission, George Müller's work for orphans, William Booth's work in the Salvation Army, and the establishment of the Moody Bible Institute in Chicago, among many other mission works that bore eternal fruit. Not long after he had given the majority of his money away, he became engaged to a woman who was just as passionate about Christ as he was. He had a few thousand pounds left to his name, and offered it to his new bride as a bit of security as they began their new life together. But she said to C. T., "Charlie, what did the Lord tell the rich young man to do?"

"Sell all," he replied.

"Well then, we will start clear with the Lord at our wedding."[9]

The young couple then sent a letter to William Booth, founder of the Salvation Army, enclosing a check for all their remaining funds, and stating, "Henceforth our bank is in heaven. . . . This step has been taken not without most definite reference to God's Word, and the command of the Lord Jesus, who said, 'Sell all that ye have and give alms. Make for yourself purses which wax not old.' . . . We can also thank God by His grace that we have not done this by constraint, but cheerfully and of a ready mind and willing heart."[10]

Imagine starting off a marriage by giving away everything you have. (What an incredibly different mind-set from most young couples today, who wouldn't dream of starting a new life together without at least some money in the bank!) But because C. T. and his wife staked all their hopes in the bank of heaven and took God at His word, their needs were always supernaturally met. Their hearts were not divided by the "deceitfulness of riches" and the "cares of this world" (see Mk. 4:19), and as a result they became one of the greatest missionary couples of their generation, impacting China, India, and later Africa in a powerful and truly world-changing way.

While God may not call every one of us to literally give up all of our possessions as He did C. T. Studd, He certainly asks each of us to sell all in a spiritual sense. In other words, when we give our lives to Jesus Christ, our money is no longer ours to do with as we choose. Everything we have now belongs to Him. Our money is at His disposal. We are to hold our possessions with an open, surrendered hand and dedicate them to be used for His purposes and for His glory. Leonard Ravenhill once said, "What does it mean to be a Christian? You have no time of your own, no money of your own—Christ must become your complete Master."[11] This must be the attitude of our hearts.

If you are clinging to your material possessions instead of freely offering them to Christ, or if financial pursuits have divided your heart from Him, ask God for the grace to surrender your money and your financial goals to Him. Ask Him to show you specific ways in which you can begin to "lay up . . . treasures in heaven" (see Mt. 6:20) instead of investing in the fleeting comforts of this earthly life. Spend some time studying Christ's words about money in Luke 12:15, John 12:3-8, Luke 18:18-25, and Matthew 6:19-33. Ask Him to shift your perspective on money from the shallow, selfish attitudes of the world to the selfless, surrendered attitude of heaven.

This may mean that you should generously give away your money, as God directs. Or it may mean that you should become more Christ-centered and purposeful with the money that you keep, no longer using it for selfish purposes, but kingdom ones. It also may mean that you should rethink your financial ambitions and career pursuits. If your decisions are directed by the desire for money rather than by the Spirit of God, you will certainly veer away from His purposes for your life and future. Let God show you what having an undivided heart in the area of money means for you specifically. If you listen with ears that are willing to hear, He will certainly direct your steps.

If Christ feels distant, if the Word of God seems empty, and if your Christianity feels flat, more than likely your heart is divided from Him because of idolatry. A key part of becoming a set-apart woman for Christ is forsaking all "other lovers" and embracing an undivided heart for Him. When you truly make Jesus your "all in all" then you will no longer wallow in disillusionment toward God or wonder what's really so special about the Christian life. Rather, you will experience joy, peace, happiness, and perfect fulfillment, even in the darkest of circumstances.

There may be areas of idolatry in your life beyond the things mentioned in this chapter. Prayerfully ask God to reveal anything you are clinging to or finding your identity in outside of Him. And then be willing to do whatever it takes to put Him first, not just with your mouth, but in every single area of your life. Think of what He has done for you. He has given everything for you. Will you not give Him everything in return?

LET'S TALK ABOUT IT

Group Study and Discussion

1. **READ JEREMIAH 29:13 AND HOSEA 2:13.** How does idolatry divide our hearts from Christ?

2. **READ LUKE 4:7-8.** What are some of the most common areas of idolatry in our culture? Why do we as Christians often excuse a preoccupation with these things in our daily lives?

TAKE IT DEEPER

Personal Study and Reflection

READ: MATTHEW 6:24

REFLECT: Do I have idolatry in my life? In what areas have I been attempting to serve two masters?

READ: ISAIAH 42:8

REFLECT: Am I willing to repent of idolatry and embrace a single-minded focus on Jesus Christ? What areas of my life must change in order for me to do this?

CHAPTER EIGHT

The Solid Rock

Exchanging Confusion for Certainty

God is not human, that he should lie, not a human being, that he should change his mind. Does he speak and then not act? Does he promise and not fulfill?

NUMBERS 23:19, NIV

We are no longer to be children, tossed here and there by waves and carried about by every wind of doctrine, by the trickery of men, by craftiness in deceitful scheming.

EPHESIANS 4:14, NASB

God's viewpoint is sometimes different from ours—so different that we could not even guess at it unless He had given us a Book which tells us such things.

CORRIE TEN BOOM, *The Hiding Place*

This Book had to be written by one of three people: good men, bad men or God. It couldn't have been written by good men because they said it was inspired by the revelation of God. Good men don't lie and deceive. It couldn't have been written by bad men because bad men would not write something that would condemn themselves. It leaves only one conclusion. It was given by divine inspiration of God.

JOHN WESLEY

ABOUT FIFTEEN YEARS AGO, Eric and I sat across from each other at our kitchen table, grappling with the realization that we had lost nearly everything we had. We'd just discovered that a dishonest employee had robbed our ministry of all its resources and that there was little to no chance of recovering what had been lost. We suddenly had no money to pay our staff or take care of our own needs, and it looked as if it might be years before we could get back on our feet.

As we made a list of everything we could sell in order to survive, I was reeling with shock and despair. How could God have let this happen? His Word said that He would never leave or forsake me and that He was my Provider, but that certainly didn't feel true in light of what we were going through. I had never really questioned God's promises. But now I found myself struggling with doubt toward God and wondering whether the Bible really meant what it said.

Eric and I somehow weathered that storm and got back on our feet financially. But for several years after that crisis happened, trials and difficulties would plunge me into depression. Spiritually speaking, I couldn't see which end was up. I felt like I was standing on unstable ground. I began to question God's love for me and to wallow in confusion. Trials only drove me further away from Him and made me feel uncertain about God's promises. I would try to work through my confusion by talking with others or seeking advice through self-help books or counseling. While I sometimes received a good suggestion here or there, I never found the unshakable clarity I was craving.

Finally, after I had spent many years repeatedly returning to this discouraging pattern, God awakened Eric and me to a principle that altered the way we responded to difficulties: *Accept God's Truth as fact and command your feelings to agree with it.* Whenever we were hit with confusion, uncertainty, or difficulties, we began to search the Word of God for answers. And when we found them, we learned to reckon them as fact, no matter what our current feelings, past experiences, or present circumstances might say. Learning to reckon God's Word as fact has revolutionized our lives and given us victory, even in our most difficult situations.

For example, as I mentioned earlier, there have been times when we've been falsely accused and threatened by people we once trusted. In those times, the emotions of fear (What if they act upon their threats?), doubt (If they hate me so much, does God still love me?), and confusion (Why would God allow this to happen?) are extremely loud. But we have become confident that we will gain clear, heavenly perspective by taking time to deliberately put "rock beneath our feet" by standing on the Truth of God's Word.

To answer the fearful question "What if they act upon their threats?" we remember the promises of God's protection in Scripture such as "no weapon formed against you shall prosper" and "with favor You will surround [the righteous] as with a shield" (Is. 54:17; Ps. 5:12). The more the voice of fear seeks to distract us, the more we meditate upon the reality that we are under the shadow of His wings. And soon, our fear is replaced with peace.

To answer the question "If they hate me so much, does God still love me?" we remember that being falsely accused for Christ's sake is actually an honor and a cause for rejoicing (see Lk. 6:22-23). And even though we may be tempted to doubt God's love for us when false accusation comes our way, we choose to stand upon the fact that His Word says the opposite. And soon, our doubt is replaced with faith.

To answer the question "Why would God allow this to happen?" we remember promises such as "all things work together for good" (Ro. 8:28) and what the Enemy means for evil, God means for good (see Gen. 50:20). We begin to stand firm upon the reality that God will turn everything that the Enemy means to harm us into something that will bless and benefit us, even if we can't see the end of the story right away. And soon, our confusion is replaced with clear heavenly perspective.

We have learned that we cannot wait for our feelings to agree with Scripture before taking it as fact. Rather, we accept God's Truth as fact and command our feelings to agree with it. When we do, our circumstances and our emotions align with the Truth of God's Word. Eric and I have applied this principle for many years, and we are no longer like infants being "tossed back and forth by the waves, and blown here and there by every wind of teaching and by the cunning and craftiness of people in their deceitful scheming" (Eph. 4:14, NIV). Confusion is gone, and certainty reigns in our hearts and minds. Why? Because we have rock beneath our feet.

RETURNING TO THE ROCK

It's amazing how tempting it can be to run anywhere but to God's Word whenever we are struggling with doubt and confusion. We think we'll find comfort and perspective in the words and ideas of our fellow humans instead of in the eternal Word of God. But human thoughts and ideas are only beneficial if they are in harmony with the timeless Truth of Scripture. All other ideas, notions, concepts, and suggestions are worthless.

If you can learn to stand upon the solid rock of God's Word in every situation you face, you will not be vulnerable to the distortion of Truth so common today. When you are exposed to ideas that do not agree with Scripture, you will be much quicker to recognize and renounce them. And when the Enemy tries to bait you with confusion, doubt, or despair, you will have a means to finding the clarity and heavenly perspective you need.

Wallowing in doubt, confusion, and uncertainty has become hip and trendy in many Christian circles. Some churches even host what they call Doubt Nights, where everyone gets together and vents their doubts about God and His Word. Confusion is celebrated today. But what a miserable way to live! Why would you choose to look at a sunset through a filthy window when you could see it in all its breathtaking beauty by looking through a sparkling clean window instead?

Remember, when we reject God's Word, we are rejecting

Jesus. He is the Word of God made flesh (see Jn. 1:1-5). He is the solid Rock upon which we must stand. Everything else in this life is uncertain, but His Word remains steadfast and immovable. He said, "Heaven and earth shall pass away, but my words shall not pass away" (Mt. 24:35, KJV). All other ground is truly sinking sand.

MAKING THE EXCHANGE

If you are being blown here and there by every wind of teaching and are overwhelmed by doubt and confusion, God is ready to plant your feet firmly upon the solid, immovable Rock, which is Jesus Christ Himself (see 1 Cor. 10:4). He is willing to replace your confusion with glorious clarity—if you are willing to take Him at His word.

Here are some practical steps that can help you get there.

1. AVOID MUSHY *Thinking*

A few years ago I listened to a radio interview (argument, rather) between a conservative Christian show host and a popular postmodern pastor. They discussed, among other things, the question of whether non-believers would really go to hell when they die. The show host was strong in his position of the biblical view of hell, but the postmodern pastor stated that he didn't believe hell was an actual place. When asked to elaborate on what he thought "hell" really was, the postmodern pastor answered with a confusing diatribe that would have baffled even the most brilliant of philosophers.

Sadly, this kind of postmodern, mushy thinking (known in some circles as "emergent Christianity") has crept into the church on a large scale and is influencing the way many people approach the Word of God today. Mushy "Christian" messages have become common: messages that imply we can never be certain about what the Bible really means, and that there is no such thing as absolute Truth. If our feet do not remain planted firmly upon the solid rock of God's Word, we will be susceptible to embracing their erroneous ideas and becoming weighed down by doubt and confusion.

Mushy thinkers will often make statements like, "none of us really can be sure about anything," and "we all have different feelings and ideas about truth; none of us is right, none of us is wrong." They do not see God's Word as solid rock upon which to stand. Rather, as they will readily admit, they view Truth as springy and undefined. These postmodern influencers are skilled at promoting confusion and doubt under the banner of "Truth." They introduce their ideas using artistry and philosophical dialogues. They often have a kind, humble, and approachable demeanor, which causes many Christians to trust them. But their creatively packaged, mushy approach toward Truth often leads to a disturbing result . . . to cause us to question what God has said.

When postmodernists examine truths from God's Word, such as Jesus being the only way to salvation, they will often pose thought-provoking questions such as, "Did God *really* say that?" and "Does God *really* mean that?"

This practice of constantly questioning the certainty of God's Word is literally sweeping over Christianity today, influencing our books, our music, the messages from our pulpits, and our daily lives. Even churches that don't claim to be "emergent" or "postmodern" often accept the idea that questioning God's Word is a wise and responsible way to grapple with Truth. And therein lies the danger.

Just think about those phrases, "Did God *really* say that?" and "Does God *really* mean that?" Do they remind you of anything? What about that scene in the book of Genesis, when Satan slithered up to Eve at the Tree of Knowledge of Good and Evil? He said to Eve, "*Did God really say,* 'You must not eat from any tree in the garden'?" (Gen. 3:1, NIV, emphasis added).

Or how about that question "Does God *really* mean that?" Kind of sounds like Satan again a few verses later when he told Eve, in essence, "No, no. You've got it all wrong! That's not really what God meant. He didn't mean 'You will surely die.' What He actually meant was . . ." (see Gen. 3:4-5).

Satan convinced Eve to question God's unchanging nature and to wonder whether He really meant what He said. He deceived her with his subtlety. He didn't brashly tell her, "You should disobey God!" Rather, through cunning and creativity, he stripped away the solid rock of Truth beneath her feet and replaced it with springy, moldable mushiness.

Tragically, he is doing the same today through the mushy postmodern ideas that have crept into the church. Many people are stumbling around in confusion, mushiness, and doubt because they have been pausing to listen to the Serpent's insipid questions and doubting whether God really meant what He said.

Since postmodern messages are highly feelings-based (for example, "How do I feel about this?" rather than "What does God say about this?"), we as women are especially prone to falling for them. Postmodern messages often appeal to our natural inclination toward love, mercy, and acceptance, using arguments such as, "Do you think that a loving God would actually send people to hell?" or, "Do you think that a merciful God would actually practice 'child abuse' by sending His only Son to die a brutal death for a crime He didn't even commit?"

The Enemy strategically targets us, just as he targeted Eve. And if we do not remain staunch in our position that the Bible means exactly what it says, we will fall for the same deception that she did.

To replace doubt with certainty, you must settle this crucial truth in your heart once and for all: *All God's Word is unchanging.* The Bible is not meant to morph and shift in order to jibe with the constantly changing culture or fit with our own preferences. The Bible is the solid rock that never alters. It was not inspired by "good men" but by the Spirit of God (see 2 Tim. 3:16). We are not to question God's Word; we are to live by it. As Jesus said, "Man shall not live by bread alone, but by every word that proceeds from the mouth of God" (Mt. 4:4).

So if you hear a mushy approach toward His Word, His promises, or His nature, run the other way, without pausing to consider the Serpent's insipid lies. Instead of listening to voices that promote doubt and uncertainty, fill your mind with truths that build your faith in God and in His unchanging Word. Read stories of the many great Christian heroes (see the Recommended Resources section beginning on page 241) who saw God's promises fulfilled in their lives time and time again. Spend time with faith-filled Christians who believe the Bible and can testify to God's faithfulness in their lives.

Ask God to make you like the wise man who built his house upon the rock, instead of the foolish man who built his house upon sand (see Mt. 7:24-27). Then, when the wind and waves of trials beat against your life, you will not be shaken, because you will be standing firmly upon a foundation that cannot be moved.

2. EXCHANGE AN OPEN MIND FOR A *Canon Mind*

There is a lot of talk these days about being open-minded. Having an open mind means being willing to entertain other people's beliefs and ideas, and even to adopt them as your own if they feel right to you. Not being open-minded puts you in the category of being closed-minded, stiff, and stodgy, not to mention unloving and judgmental. Why would any of us want to take on that kind of label?

But in order to have our feet planted firmly upon the solid Rock of Christ, we must look to the Truth of God's Word as the lens through which we evaluate the validity of any human thought, idea, belief, or philosophy. Does that mean we are to be close-minded—never willing to hear another person's ideas, always having to be right and staunchly holding our position in a prideful, arrogant way? No. We must exchange an open mind, not for a closed mind, but for a canon mind. (*Canon* simply means the sixty-six books of Scripture.)

Having a canon mind means that you implicitly trust God's definition of reality, are exclusively devoted to God's opinions and commands, and are closed to all thoughts, ideas, or philosophies that promote any reality other than His. The canon mind is built upon the conviction that God's Word is the perfect revelation of fact, that it cannot lie, and that it is 100 percent Truth. When you have a canon mind, you know that God intends His Word to be comprehended, understood, and lived out by His saints. When you have a canon mind, you are not open to any thought or definition of reality that is not 100 percent concurrent with the revelation of God's Word.

How do you develop a canon mind? As we have already discussed, it begins with the decision to take God's Word as fact. If God said it, and He cannot lie, then there is nothing more to argue. Once you have settled it in your heart that Scripture *is* Truth and that the Bible's message *is* reality, the next step is to *know and love* the Word of God. Too many of us are susceptible to error because we are ignorant of what the Bible actually says. Set aside some time each day to study and meditate upon God's Word. Learn how to explore Scripture and delve deep into God's meaning behind every verse. Use tools such as inductive Bible study courses and Bible websites such as www.blueletterbible.org that can help you learn to use concordances and study the Greek and Hebrew roots of each word in the Bible. Download an audio version of the Bible (we personally like *The Word of Promise*) and listen to it around the house, in your car, and even while you are falling asleep at night. Spend time around other believers who reverence and love the Word of God. Talk about what you are learning in Scripture and listen to what they are learning. Ask God's Spirit to make His timeless Word come alive to you.

As you begin to make God's Word the foundation of your life, practice applying specific truths, commands, and promises to situations you face each day. Memorize some key verses to help you immediately combat lies with Truth. For instance, if you struggle with the temptation to hold on to offenses, memorize verses such as "[love] is not easily angered" (1 Cor. 13:5, NIV) or "Be kind and compassionate to one another, forgiving each other, just as in Christ God forgave you" (Eph. 4:32, NIV). (Yes, the enabling power of God will equip you to live out these commands, but you can't live out God's Truth if you don't first know what it is!) No matter what your circumstances or struggles, you can *always* find an answer in the Word of God. If you cannot find one immediately, begin to search for it as if you were searching for hidden treasure, and ask God to guide you as you look to His Truth for answers.

For a beautiful and inspiring vision of the way we are to interact with God's Word, take some time to read through Psalm 119. As you fall in love with Scripture and cultivate a canon mind, you will soon find yourself standing upon a Rock that cannot be moved.

3. PUT FEELINGS IN *Their Place*

Among the most popular messages of our society today is the proclamation "Follow your heart!" The culture has conditioned us to place a high value on our own desires and emotions. We are encouraged to base both our major life decisions and lifestyle choices upon how we feel. "Don't know what to do? Just listen to your heart! Do what feels right to you!" This advice permeates everything from love songs to children's movies.

But God gives us different directions when it comes to our hearts and emotions: "He who trusts in his own heart is a fool" (Prov. 28:26) and "The heart is deceitful above all things" (Jer. 17:9).

As attractive as the "follow your heart" message may seem, adopting this mind-set can be toxic to our spiritual lives. When we allow our emotions and whims to lead us, we become subservient to our feelings rather than to God's Spirit and His Word. Following our heart cultivates an attitude of selfishness rather than one of surrender. We cannot become the bondservants of Christ if we are controlled by our feelings.

Elisabeth Elliot said this about putting emotions in their place: "[We must] keep a tight rein on our emotions. They may remain, but it is not they who are to rule the action. They have no authority. A life lived in God is not lived on the plane of the feelings, but of the will."[1]

When we don't live on the "plane of the will," our feelings lead the way, and we become prone to "picking and choosing" our Truth, receiving the things that make us feel good and rejecting the things that don't. When we accept only the parts of God's Truth that appeal to us, and dismiss all the rest, we cannot receive the "whole counsel of God" (see Acts 20:27) and we end up with a distorted "truth" of our own making. (That is why so many of our churches today promote a soft, flimsy Gospel instead of a powerful, life-transforming one.)

Even those of us who believe in the inerrancy of Scripture have often been conditioned to consult "feelings first" when grappling with Truth. When we are deciding whether to believe God's promises or obey His commands, we often ask ourselves, "How do I feel about this?" rather than, "What does God say about this?"

It bears repeating: God's Truth is unchanging, and He cannot lie (see Titus 1:2). Our emotions and personal experiences may not always line up with the commands and promises of the Bible. But does that make His Word any less true? When we try to edit Truth to mesh with our own emotions or preferences, we are placing our own opinions and thoughts higher than God's. It doesn't matter how we feel about what God says, and it also doesn't matter what our past experience states. If our feelings and experiences don't match up with God's Word, the fault lies with us, not Him. As it says in Romans 3:4, "Let God be true but every man a liar."

Responses like the following indicate that we are using our experience to determine the reliability of Scripture: "But

I prayed for such and such, and God didn't come through for me, and now I can't trust Him or believe His promises." Or, "The Bible talks about peace and joy, but all I've ever experienced is despair and heartache!"

God cares deeply about each one of your painful past experiences and each one of your current struggles. We must always remember that *receiving* His Truth, not running away from it, is what leads to clarity and victory. The answers and reasons why may not always be clear. But if you learn to place His unchanging, eternal Truth far above your own feelings and experiences, you will soon begin to experience freedom, faith, and heavenly perspective beyond what you ever thought possible.

When we Christians evaluate Truth on the plane of emotion and experience, rather than on the solid rock of God's Word, we end up with the muddled postmodern thinking so common in the church today. But when the timeless Word of God is our baseline for reasoning, we find clarity, purpose, and passion in knowing exactly what we believe and why. (For more on this subject, I encourage you to listen to the message "The Anatomy of Faith" available for free download at www.ellerslie.com.)

4. DON'T PLACE ART OVER *Truth*

The arts are an enormous part of any culture, and Christians have long sought to experience and express God through music, poetry, allegory, art, and specific environments (whether artsy coffee shops or inspiring cathedrals). While

God can certainly be expressed and experienced through all of these mediums, all too many Christians have begun to place a higher value on art than on Truth. Postmodernists love to use artistry to define their Christianity, stating that movies, art, poetry, and atmosphere speak to their souls about God far more than the Bible does. All too often, the erosion of Truth is being justified under the banner of artistic license and self-expression. A common mind-set toward anything artistic in the church today is as follows:

Angst is hip. If I think a thought, no matter if the thought contradicts and challenges all the traditional moorings and moral building blocks of a Judeo-Christian worldview, I should entertain the thought, speak it, paint it, put melody to it, sing it, write it, put it in prose, and/or even sculpt it.

Go with it. If I feel a feeling, a longing, or an urge, no matter if the feeling (longing or urge) violates that which has been taught me as proper in the biblical framework, I should express it, yell it, indulge it, embrace it, and/or cultivate it.

Self is central. If I don't let the thoughts, feelings, longings, and urges out, I am repressing my real, true self. And my real, true self must get out, it must be known, it must be expressed.

We often think of artistic expression as a safe medium for us to let out all our pent-up feelings and express our true selves. Christians who feel this way don't evaluate their artistic expressions in light of God's Truth, but in light of their own emotions and ideas. They may conduct themselves as conservative Christians at church or at Bible study, but on their blog, or in their music, or in their art, they let their guard down under the banner of artistic freedom.

But diminishing Truth under the banner of artistic expression is a counterfeit form of freedom. Jesus said, "You shall know the truth, and the truth shall make you free. . . . If the Son makes you free, you shall be free indeed" (Jn. 8:32,36). And the psalmist David declared, "I will walk at liberty, *for I seek Your precepts*" (Ps. 119:45, emphasis added).

True freedom comes from agreeing with God's Truth, not disregarding it. So if you are involved in any form of art— whether it be music, writing, poetry, photography, painting, or anything else—make sure that the message you are conveying through these mediums lines up with God's Word, 100 percent. That doesn't mean that every word you write or photo you take has to specifically be *about* God, but it should always *reflect* Him: His nature, His love, His holiness, and His Truth.

Henry Ward Beecher said, "If a man cannot be a Christian in the place where he is, he cannot be a Christian anywhere."[2] By the same token, if a woman cannot be a Christian in her artistic expressions, she cannot be a Christian anywhere.

This principle must also apply to the artistic mediums

we choose to listen to, read, and participate in. Just because a musician calls himself a Christian artist doesn't mean his music expresses God's nature and His Truth. And just because someone has a Christian blog doesn't mean it is going to point you to Jesus Christ. Be on guard against artistic messages that diminish "the whole counsel of God" and exalt cultural notions over biblical fact (see Acts 20:27).

It is also important to be watchful of adopting art-over-Truth mind-sets, such as "The Bible doesn't speak to me, but movies do" or "I can't feel close to God unless I'm in an inspiring environment like an artsy coffee shop." If you do not believe you can experience God except through artistic mediums, then you are not seeking the God of the Bible. He says, "'Heaven is My throne, and earth is My footstool. Where is the house that you will build Me? And where is the place of My rest? For all those things My hand has made . . . ,' says the LORD. 'But . . . [I will look] on him who is poor and of a contrite spirit, and who trembles at My word'" (Is. 66:1-2).

Do you want to find the one true God? Finding Him is a simple matter of humbling yourself before Him and trembling at His Word.

Not long ago in a persecuted nation, a group of believers was gathered together for a secret Bible study when police officers burst in and took over the meeting. They rounded up all the Christians, and one by one they pointed a gun to each person's head, threatening to kill him or her unless the person spit on the Bible. With heavy hearts, each member of the group took turns spitting on the cover of the Bible in order to preserve their lives. But one sixteen-year-old girl, with tears streaming down her face, tenderly wiped the spittle from the Bible with the corner of her dress. A few seconds later, she was dead.[3]

Throughout history, men and women have given up their lives to protect the purity of Scripture. In light of their astounding sacrifices, it is heartbreaking to see countless American Christians disregarding and questioning God's Word.

In this day and age where "truth is fallen in the street" (Is. 59:14), God is looking for courageous, set-apart Christians who are willing to wipe the spit from His precious Word, no matter what it may cost them. Will you be counted among them? (To go deeper into this subject I encourage you to listen to the messages "The Evil Side of Artistic" and "Betrayed with a Kiss," available for free download at www.ellerslie.com.)

LET'S TALK ABOUT IT

Group Study and Discussion

1. READ NUMBERS 23:19. Why is it dangerous to question the Word of God?

2. READ MATTHEW 7:24-25. Is God's Truth meant to be mushy and uncertain, or a solid rock upon which to build our lives? When we take God's Word as fact, how does it impact our spiritual lives?

TAKE IT DEEPER

Personal Study and Reflection

READ: EPHESIANS 4:14

REFLECT: Have I been influenced by postmodern thinking? How has this impacted my relationship with Christ?

READ: 2 CORINTHIANS 1:19-20

REFLECT: Have I been evaluating God's Word based on my own feelings, or have I been taking it as fact? Am I willing to put aside my feelings and experiences, and simply rest upon the fact that God has said it and He cannot lie? How will this attitude affect my spiritual life?

CHAPTER NINE

Strong and Courageous

Exchanging Anxiety for Confidence

Strength and dignity are her clothing, and she smiles at the future.

PROVERBS 31:25, NASB

Have I not commanded you? Be strong and of good courage; do not be afraid, nor be dismayed, for the LORD your God is with you wherever you go.

JOSHUA 1:9

Worrying is carrying tomorrow's load with today's strength—carrying two days at once. It is moving into tomorrow ahead of time. Worrying doesn't empty tomorrow of its sorrow, it empties today of its strength.

CORRIE TEN BOOM

I am no longer anxious about anything, as I realize that He is able to carry out His will for me. It does not matter where He places me, or how. That is for Him to consider, not me, for in the easiest positions He will give me grace, and in the most difficult ones, His grace is sufficient.

J. HUDSON TAYLOR

E RIC AND I HAD been in full-time ministry for about two years when I started waking up in the night with panic attacks. One minute I would be peacefully sleeping, and the next I'd be sitting straight up in bed, my heart pounding, my hands shaking, my breathing short and shallow. Fear, worry, stress, and anxiety seemed to overtake my every thought. No matter how much willpower I exerted, foreboding and dread kept washing over my mind and emotions like a tidal wave. It usually took several hours before I calmed down enough to get back to sleep. Once I even ended up in the emergency room at 2:00 a.m. because my symptoms of anxiety were so extreme I wondered if I might be having a heart attack.

Fear had begun to control my life. Even my days were becoming clouded by constant worry and anxiety.

Eric and I were a young, fresh, and enthusiastic couple when we launched into the adventure of Christian ministry. But we were unprepared for the spiritual battle we had entered into. The stress of being in the public eye combined with the spiritual intensity of being in ministry had begun to take a toll on us both, but especially upon me. I became so riddled with anxiety I could hardly function.

Our marriage was strong, but it seemed that every other area of our lives was weak. Every time we tried to fulfill the call of God upon our lives, a million roadblocks seemed to stand in our way. Things like financial crisis, relational betrayal and backstabbing, exhaustion, and distressing health problems became the norm. Every time we tried to take a step forward into something God was calling us to, one of us (usually me) would be hit with some hindering and miserable sickness.

Though we saw many lives changed through the message we spoke, behind the scenes I wondered how much longer I could go on. What else was God going to take me through? How much of this did He think I could handle? Fear skewed my perspective of God and hindered my walk with Him. Subconsciously I pulled away from an intimate relationship with Him, because I no longer trusted Him with all of my heart. His Word exhorted me to have faith in His goodness and mercy, but how could I have faith when it seemed He had let me down so many times? Scripture beckoned me to "be anxious for nothing" (Phil. 4:6). But how could I banish anxiety when I was constantly bracing for the next blow?

I spent several months crying out to God for answers. *Lord,* I prayed, *show me what is standing in the way of my ability to walk in the victory, strength, joy, and peace You intended for my life.*

As I looked back over my life, I began to recognize that I had never truly been free from fear. It had been my constant companion, in one shape or another, since childhood.

It had started in elementary school.

During my second-grade year, our school gave a special teaching series called Health and Safety for Kids. Our teacher, Mrs. Jamison, taught us the importance of many valuable habits, such as toothbrushing, hand washing, and seat-belt wearing, and she warned us about stranger danger. We were told one horror story after the next about little boys and girls who were playing hopscotch on the sidewalk one moment and tied up in the trunk of a bad guy's car the next. Such accounts filled me with a deep, abiding terror of being kidnapped. I was under the impression that child snatchers were everywhere, surveying our homes, and calculating ways that they could carry me away. I started looking over my shoulder every time I went outside to play.

By the end of the Health and Safety for Kids study, I had been shaped into a responsible little girl, at least when it came to buckling up and areas of cleanliness and personal hygiene. The problem was, I had also been shaped into a fearful little girl. Before second grade, I'd never worried about dying from horrible, painful diseases (from failure to wash my hands for at least fifteen seconds), losing all my teeth (from forgetting to carefully brush in circles on both top and bottom), or flying into oblivion (from failing to "buckle up for safety!"). Second grade had made me paranoid about many what-ifs that I'd never thought about before.

If my mom ever left me in our station wagon while she went to an ATM kiosk to withdraw cash, I would shut my eyes tightly and pray frantically that the kidnappers wouldn't smash the car window to grab me in the sixty seconds she was gone. When I accompanied my parents to the supermarket, I clung to their pant legs, afraid to let go for even one moment, lest the child stalkers seize me and whisk me out of the store.

After about two years of nightmares and self-imposed kidnapping-prevention tactics, I moved beyond my paranoia and functioned a bit more normally around strangers. But from that point on, I was never free from fear. It just took on different forms, depending on what season of life I was in.

In middle school, I was terrified of being humiliated in front of my peers and was obsessed with dressing in the latest trends, being up to speed on the cool words to use, and avoiding being seen in public with my parents or younger siblings. In high school, fears about my grades and studies plagued me, causing me to spend countless hours cramming for tests and worrying about my academic future.

As I entered my adult years, I struggled with anxiety over my health, relationships, and the future. The what-if questions that I'd learned to ask in second grade seemed to follow me year after year: *What if I fail this class? What if all my friends turn against me? What if I never get married? What if my health falls apart and I die prematurely?*

When I reflected back upon the leading role that fear had played throughout my life, I was ashamed to admit that I had spent countless days, weeks, and even years plagued and distracted by the possibilities of all the bad things that might happen to me.

Though my fears calmed a bit during my engagement and early months of marriage, as soon as I started experiencing the trials and challenges of full-time Christian ministry, fear began to rear its ugly head again, in a more intense way than ever before.

I didn't know why I was enslaved to fear. I only knew I couldn't continue living this way. I spent months praying and crying out to God for freedom from the bondage of fear, and then He answered that cry of my heart, more faithfully and fully than I ever could have imagined. Gently and lovingly, He opened my eyes to see His face more clearly and understand His nature like never before. And in the process, He armed me with a measure of strength and triumph I never knew He intended me to have.

MAKING THE EXCHANGE

In the following pages, I'd like to walk you through the journey God took me on to overcome fear. If you are ready to experience the victory and strength He has for you as a set-apart woman, I encourage you to walk through these steps in your own life.

1. PUT ON THE *Armor of God*

It never occurred to Eric or me that some of the trials we were facing might be attacks from the Enemy. We saw countless promises in the Bible about the bountiful blessings of God, but we assumed that we should not expect this abundance and supernatural provision in every area of life. After all, there are plenty of Scriptures about God disciplining His children and taking them through trials. So we figured that the difficulty, stress, and chaos in our lives were things He was allowing in order to teach us patience and dependence.

But as I prayed about the fierce attacks upon my life, God opened my eyes to the fact that the hits were not coming from Him; they were coming from the enemy of my soul. God did not want me to resign myself to accepting these attacks. Rather, He wanted me to call upon His name and allow Him to come to my rescue.

James 4:7 says, "Resist the devil and he will flee from you." I hadn't been resisting the Enemy's blows, because I had assumed they were coming from God, or at least being allowed by God for the purpose of discipline. Yet, when I thought about it, I realized that the result in my spiritual life wasn't the life-giving victory God's loving discipline brings. Instead, it was the despair and discouragement that the Enemy brings. I had always thought that the most God-pleasing thing I could do when bad things happened was to accept them and move on. But God was showing me that when the Enemy attacked, He wanted me to stand up and fight by the power of His Spirit.

I had been attributing something to God that is contrary to His nature. Yes, God disciplines us and refines us, but not in a harsh, cruel way that brings fear and confusion into our lives. God's ways bring light and life, not darkness and death.

To become the valiant, set-apart women we are called to be, we cannot just roll over and play dead when the Enemy attacks us. We must stand firm and resist (in the mighty power of Christ's name), not allowing Satan to hinder God's purposes for our lives. As it says in Ephesians 6:10-11: "Be strong in the Lord and in the power of His might. Put on the whole armor of God, that you may be able to stand against the wiles of the devil."

Eric and I carefully studied what Scripture says about the difference between God's nature and Satan's nature so that we would better understand which trials were coming from the Enemy and which were coming from God. As we identified the areas of enemy attack in our lives, we learned how to stand in faithful, wrestling prayer against those attacks. Going on the offensive spiritually annihilated fear and gave me confidence I never knew was possible.

Many of the great Christian women whose lives I've studied understood how to "put on the whole armor of God" (Eph. 6:11) and "extinguish all the flaming darts of the evil one" (Eph. 6:16, ESV). Here's a case in point.

When Gladys Aylward was a young missionary on her way to China she was detained by corrupt government officials in Russia. As she sat in a hotel room, thinking about a way to escape, a man tried to force his way in.

Boldly she told him, "You are not coming in here."

"Why not?" he smirked.

"Because this is my bedroom."

"I am the master; I can do with you what I wish."

"Oh no, you cannot. You may not believe in God, but He is here. Touch me and see. Between you and me God has put a barrier. Go!"

The man stared at Gladys, shivered, and without another word, turned and left.[1]

Imagine having that much confidence in the protection

that God promises His children! Not just *hoping* God will come through for us, but *knowing* He will. Not cowering when the Enemy tries to attack, but rising up in the strength of God and trampling him under our feet.

Christ has already conquered the enemy of our souls. The only thing Satan can do is put on a magic show, using smoke and mirrors to trick us into taking him seriously and letting him have his way in our lives. But if we stand firmly in the power that Christ has given us, no weapon formed against us will prosper (see Is. 54:17).

Take some time to study what Scripture says about the nature of Christ versus the nature of Satan. Make a list of any of the attacks in your life that are coming from the Enemy and not from God. Instead of accepting the harassments of the Enemy, resist his attacks, standing confident in the authority Jesus has given you. Once you recognize that you don't have to accept Satan's harassments and that Jesus Christ has given you power over the forces of darkness, you can walk boldly and confidently in your position as a protected child of the King (see Lk. 10:19).

As we trust in God's protection, we can rest in the fact that the Enemy cannot have his way in our lives (see Lk. 10:19; Jas. 4:7). Yet this doesn't mean that God will never allow us to face difficulties, or that we won't walk through "trials of many kinds" (see Jas. 1:2, NIV), such as persecution or false accusation. However, when trials and difficulties come, we can trust that God will give us the courage we need, right when we need it.

In her book *The Hiding Place*, Corrie ten Boom tells a story from her childhood that beautifully illustrates this principle. One day she confided to her father that she feared she would never have the courage to face hardship and suffering.

> "Corrie," he began gently. "When you and I go to Amsterdam—when do I give you your ticket?"
>
> "Why, just before we get on the train," she replied.
>
> "Exactly. And our wise Father in heaven knows when we're going to need things, too. Don't run out ahead of him, Corrie. When the time comes [for you to suffer], you will look into your heart and find the strength you need—just in time."[2]

Fretting and worrying about what-ifs shows a lack of trust in our God. We envision all the possible trials we might face, but we fail to look at them through a heavenly lens and remember the grace, strength, and victory that God offers for every challenge we must walk through. God gives us the grace we need for specific trials right when we need it, and not before.

Rather than worrying about what might happen in the future, we can rest in the knowledge that:

- God can turn anything the Enemy means for evil into good in our lives (see Gen. 50:20; Ro. 8:28).

- He will not allow us to walk through trials we are not able to handle (see 1 Cor. 10:13).
- Even when we walk through difficult circumstances, we can triumph through every challenge when we put our hope in Him (see Ps. 25:3).

Not only is worrying about what-ifs dangerous to our spiritual lives, but it also distracts us from "being all there" for the work God has called us to today. Elisabeth Elliot wrote,

Today's care, not tomorrow's, is the responsibility given to us, apportioned in the wisdom of God. Often we neglect the thing assigned for the moment because we are preoccupied with something that is not our business just now. How easy it is to give only half our attention to someone who needs us . . . because the other half is focused on a future worry.[3]

When we lay down our worries at Jesus' feet and take up the shield of faith to resist the Enemy, we'll experience the "strength for today and bright hope for tomorrow"[4] that God intends us to have.

2. *Forsake* THE WORLDLY "WISDOM" OF FEAR

Our culture constantly bombards us with the message that being fearful is equivalent to being wise. For instance, we should be worried about money and career, or else we might end up in a homeless shelter. We should be obsessed with finding the right guy, or else we might end up sad and alone for the rest of our lives. We should be consumed with health, exercise, and dieting, or else we'll die young from obesity or heart failure.

At least that's what our culture wants us to believe. But in reality, fear does not bring freedom. It only brings imprisonment.

Young women are often so fearful of being single that they continually strategize how to dress and act in order to get the opposite sex to notice them. Others are so stressed about having a secure financial future that they nearly kill themselves trying to climb the corporate ladder. Moms are obsessed with all the latest studies about which electronics could be giving off harmful radiation and which kinds of toys could cause their kids to get lead poisoning. The more knowledge they gain about what might harm them or their families, the more paranoid and self-protective they become.

Who has time for real intimacy with Jesus Christ when we have so many urgent, important issues to worry about?

I know these pitfalls all too well. Throughout my years in bondage to fear, I developed many self-protective tendencies designed to barricade my life from trials and discomfort. Along the way, I somehow convinced myself that in doing so, I was being wise and responsible.

As I shared earlier, in order to protect my health, I took piles of supplements every day and put myself in bondage to all kinds of dietary restrictions. To protect my emotions, I would slip away after speaking events to avoid being

drained by the many young women who wanted to ask me
for advice. To protect my reputation, I avoided speaking
Truth as straightforwardly as I knew God wanted me to. To
protect my privacy, I became reluctant to open my home
to strangers or practice hospitality. To protect our finances,
I remained in a constant state of frantic busyness, stressing
about one urgent task after the next. And the list went on
and on.

God showed me that that I was using up a lot of hours
on fear and selfishness; I was turning inward and becoming
preoccupied with my own happiness, well-being, and protection. I had learned to build life around my own health,
comfort, and security instead of living for Jesus Christ and
joyfully embracing His call to turn outward and sacrificially
serve others.

Though the world's wisdom says, "It's your responsibility
to protect your own life and interests!" God's wisdom says
something entirely different: "Be anxious for nothing" (Phil.
4:6) and "Seek first the kingdom of God . . . and all these
things shall be added to you" (Mt. 6:33).

While I'm all for following sound "life principles" such as
working hard in school, taking care of our health, protecting
our children, and avoiding outright stupidity, I have come to
realize how easily fear can disguise itself as "wisdom."

Living in fear is not equivalent to living in wisdom.
Rather, living in fear is living in direct disobedience to God.
He doesn't just suggest that we "fear not." Instead, He com-
mands us not to fear:

Have I not commanded you? Be strong and courageous.
Do not be afraid; do not be discouraged, for the LORD
your God will be with you wherever you go.

(JOSH. 1:9, NIV)

As Sarah obeyed Abraham, calling him lord, whose
daughters you are if you do good and are not afraid
with any terror.

(1 PET. 3:6)

We must begin to recognize fear for what it really is: sin.

When I finally understood this, I repented of my sin and
asked God to reshape my habits in these areas. Instead of
taking my cues from the latest studies, the newest books, or
the advice of secular magazines, I began to turn to His Word
for wisdom on how to eat, how to practice hospitality, how
to approach finances, and how to invest in the lives of others.

What a difference it made! As I learned to tune out the
world's advice and instead focus on Jesus and His priorities for my life, I was set free from the debilitating need to
barricade and self-protect. It became my joy and delight to
embrace the call of God upon my life, knowing that He
would protect my health, finances, and emotions as I built
my life around Him. Yes, I still sought to make sound decisions in areas such as health and finances, but my security
no longer came from my own self-protection or the advice
of the world. Rather, it came from simple, childlike faith in
my faithful God.

Prayerfully ask God to awaken you to any areas of your life in which you are living in fear and self-protection, yet calling it wisdom. Ask Him to reshape your attitudes and habits in these areas. Practice turning to the Word of God instead of to worldly or ungodly counsel, and build your decisions around His wisdom instead of this world's. Instead of clinging self-protectively to your life, health, finances, and comforts, ask for the grace to completely entrust those areas of your life to Jesus Christ. When you do, you will discover a tremendous freedom from the bondage of fear.

3. TAKE FEARFUL THOUGHTS *Captive*

Martin Luther once said, "You can't stop the birds from flying over your head, but you can keep them from building a nest in your hair." We may not be able to keep fearful thoughts from entering our minds, but we can kick them out the moment they arrive so that they don't take root inside our hearts and control our lives. That is the essence of 2 Corinthians 10:5: "Casting down arguments and every high thing that exalts itself against the knowledge of God, bringing every thought into captivity to the obedience of Christ."

In my journey to overcome fear, I slowly began to learn how to take authority over every thought entering my mind and to replace lies with Truth. If fearful thoughts about finances began to flit through my mind, such as *I wonder if our finances will be able to handle all these unexpected bills? What if we end up losing everything?* I would immediately refuse to turn those thoughts over in my mind and instead begin meditating upon God's promises for provision, such as, "My God shall supply all your need according to His riches in glory" (Phil. 4:19).

If fearful thoughts about health began to arise, such as *I wonder what that strange pain in my shoulder is—I hope it's not something serious!* I would immediately say no to those thoughts and instead dwell upon God's promises for protection and strength, such as, "No evil shall befall you, nor shall any plague come near your dwelling" (Ps. 91:10).

At first, it felt tedious and time-consuming to switch fearful thoughts to faith-filled thoughts, but the more I put this principle into practice, the more it became habitual in my life. Now, after many years of working on this discipline, it comes much more automatically.

Whenever you are tempted to dwell on fearful what-if scenarios, fill your mind with Truth instead. A great way to start this principle is by memorizing some of the Psalms. Some of my favorites are Psalm 27, 34, 37, 46, 91, and 112. Whenever you are faced with temptation to fear, those words of Truth can become vital weapons with which to chase away those thoughts. The more you fill your mind with Truth, the scarcer lies will become.

Another thing you can do is to pray for someone else when the Enemy harasses you with fearful thoughts. When we pray for someone else we take our focus off ourselves and our own fears. Prayer for others—intercessory prayer—turns us outward instead of inward.

When we know our God and believe Him to be exactly as

His Word says He is, we have no reason to let fearful thoughts overtake our minds. Ask God for the strength to take authority over fearful thoughts. Train your mind to dwell upon His reality and His Truth and develop the habit of immediately saying no to the Enemy's foreboding suggestions.

God has called each of us to valiant femininity. By His grace, we can be set free from the snares of fear and anxiety and filled with supernatural strength and courage that will cause the Enemy to flee from us. God's strength can put us on the offense, spiritually, instead of on the defense. All we must do is allow Him to build us strong in Him and to dress us in His holy armor. Remember, "God has not given us a spirit of fear, but of power and of love and of a sound mind" (2 Tim. 1:7)!

LET'S TALK ABOUT IT

Group Study and Discussion

1. READ MATTHEW 6:25-34. What is the difference between worldly wisdom and childlike faith? Why do we often choose worldly wisdom? What are the spiritual benefits of childlike faith?

2. READ PROVERBS 31:21 AND 1 PETER 3:6. Why is courage such an important part of becoming a set-apart woman? How can we cultivate godly courage in our daily lives?

TAKE IT DEEPER

Personal Study and Reflection

READ: JOSHUA 1:9

REFLECT: Have I been obeying God's command to not be afraid, or have I considered myself a victim to fear? Do I believe that God can set me free from fear by His enabling power? (If yes, take some time to lay your worries at His feet and ask Him to set you free from the bondage of fear. Write down anything He is speaking to your heart.)

READ: EPHESIANS 6:10-11

REFLECT: Have I been allowing Satan to harass me in any area of my life? Am I ready to resist him in the authority and power of Christ? How will my daily life change if I begin to resist his attacks instead of accepting them?

CHAPTER TEN

So I Send You

Exchanging Selfish Pursuits for Sacrificial Love

As the Father has sent Me, I also send you.

JOHN 20:21

Pure and undefiled religion before God and the Father is this: to visit orphans and widows in their trouble.

JAMES 1:27

It is not to make money that I believe a Christian should live. The noblest thing a man can do is, just humbly to receive, and then go amongst others and give.

DAVID LIVINGSTONE

Some wish to live within the sound of church or chapel bell. I want to run a rescue shop within a yard of hell.

C. T. STUDD

A FEW YEARS AGO, Eric and I were walking out of Whole Foods in California, when two young women holding clipboards approached us. One wore long blonde dreadlocks; the other sported a large, ornate nose ring. Their faces were intent and sincere as they asked for a moment of our time.

"We represent Greenpeace," said the blonde, "and we have an important issue that we're letting people know about today."

"That's right," the other young woman chimed in. "There are fifty humpback whales in danger right now off the coast of Japan. We are fighting for legislation that will protect them."

"It's so sad how the government is stalling on this," her friend added mournfully. "The lives of fifty animals are at stake, and they are just sitting on their thumbs. If you sign this petition, it will motivate them to action."

The girl wearing the nose ring held out her clipboard. "And if you want to give a donation, it will help toward the eighteen million dollars we are trying to raise to build a safe haven for the whales."

The two young women were so passionate about their cause that they looked close to tears. You would have thought the fifty whales were their beloved childhood pets that were about to be ruthlessly murdered. They simply could not rest until the precious creatures were saved.

Hours later, when we drove past Whole Foods again, the two women were still standing outside, pleading with everyone exiting the store to stand up and fight on behalf of the defenseless ocean creatures. I couldn't get past the irony of the situation. Only a few months earlier, Eric and I had studied the plight of orphans and vulnerable children around the world. We learned that there were 143 million orphans—children alone and without advocates, children dying of starvation and disease without anyone to rescue them. The number was so staggering that we couldn't imagine how to put a dent in it. (That number has now increased to approximately 163 million.) We'd learned that there are 27 million human slaves in the world today, a large number being young girls sold into forced prostitution. We'd heard the tragic stories of the child soldiers in Uganda and the desperate plight of the street children in South America. In light of such heartbreaking realities, passionately fighting to save fifty whales off the coast of Japan seemed nothing short of ridiculous.

I found myself wondering what would happen if I started fighting for vulnerable children with as much devotion as the Greenpeace girls put into fighting to save those humpback whales. How passionately was I willing to fight for the causes that were on God's heart? Was I willing to get out of my comfort zone and pour out my life for the weak, not just in ways that were convenient and easy but in ways that required personal sacrifice? Was I willing to not just shake my head at the suffering around the world, but to take up their cause as my own?

I was reminded of the words in Proverbs 31:8-9, "Open your mouth for the speechless, in the cause of all who are appointed to die. Open your mouth, judge righteously, and plead the cause of the poor and needy." Was I willing to open my mouth for the oppressed, the hungry, and the vulnerable lives around the world?

As young Christians, both Eric and I had gained a special heart for the vulnerable. But somewhere in the busyness of our lives, we'd let that burden fall by the wayside; we'd lost our passion to defend, fight, comfort, and rescue the weak. We were in full-time ministry and serving God, yet we were missing a key part of the Gospel: becoming Christ's hands and feet to the poor and needy.

As American believers, most of us don't give a lot of thought or energy to rescuing the orphan, the slave, and the impoverished. We don't mind "doing our Christian duty" by going on a two-week mission trip every couple of years or giving money to an orphanage fund at our church, just as long as it doesn't inconvenience us too much. But few of us are willing to fight for the cause of the vulnerable with even half as much passion and dedication as those young women showed on behalf of the fifty whales.

The Bible describes a similar attitude in the people of Sodom, before God destroyed their city: "This was the iniquity of your sister Sodom: She and her daughter had pride, fullness of food, and abundance of idleness; neither did she strengthen the hand of the poor and needy" (Ezk. 16:49).

When we become focused on ourselves and indifferent to the cry of the poor and needy, it is a serious thing in the sight of God. It is sobering to realize that on Judgment Day He will say to some of us, "Depart from Me, you cursed, into the everlasting fire prepared for the devil and his angels: for I was hungry and you gave Me no food; I was thirsty and you gave Me no drink; I was a stranger and you did not take Me in, naked and you did not clothe Me, sick and in prison and you did not visit Me" (Mt. 25:41-43).

Rees Howells, an evangelist in the early 1900s, once described a life-changing moment when he was walking through his village and praying for a sibling group of orphaned children who had recently lost their parents. *God, be a Father to the fatherless,* he prayed, quoting from Psalm 68. Immediately, he felt God's Spirit speak to his heart: "I am a Father to the fatherless, but . . . I must be one through you." Rees was challenged at that moment not to merely pray for the orphaned children, but to love them sacrificially and become a father to them.[1]

A LIFE-CHANGING MOMENT

God impressed a similar message upon Eric's heart when our son Hudson was four years old. Eric describes it this way:

I remember the day my life turned upside down. I was on the phone, interviewing a missionary from Liberia. As she described the state of this suffering country, I was moved, startled, and deeply grieved. I remember her saying, "We just need Christians to come and give their life, Eric. We have so many orphans and not enough hands and feet." She told me about a little four-year-old boy sitting on the side of the road. She said, "Eric, there are children all around us, like him, that we just can't reach. We don't have the resources, the space, or the staff. So this boy sits there starving to death without anyone to comfort him, feed him, cover him, or house him. He's dying, Eric, and it would appear that no one on earth even cares."

I cringed as I listened to her words. I really did feel bad for this boy. But it was the sort of grief that you feel over things like bad political events, stock market drops, and rumors about human trafficking in Cambodia. After the phone call, I shook my head in disbelief that such things were happening, and I prayed to God to somehow intervene on behalf of this little one. But after that, I went back to my business as usual. In the middle of that night, I was awakened. My mind was filled with a picture of that little four-year-old boy sitting on the side of the road in Liberia. And then God pressed a question into my heart: "Eric, what if that little boy was Hudson?"

I was staggered at the question. For even the thought of my son enduring such deprivation was more than my fatherly soul could handle. I didn't want to think such a thought. But the question kept booming,

"What if that was Hudson?"

Without hesitation I knew the answer to such a question. I am a father, aren't I?

If that abandoned little boy was Hudson, I would

beat through every obstacle to reach my son. There would be no delays, no second guesses, no trifling with the petty cares of the home front. I would get on the first plane that could take me to Liberia. And if I, for some reason, was paralyzed from going, I would call up everyone that calls themselves my friend and beg them to go get to my son.

God wasted no time in harpooning my soul: "Eric, that is my Hudson!"

I sat there in the dark with my face awash with shock. I saw something that I had never before seen. I saw His Father's heart for that little four-year-old boy.

It was as if He were saying, "Eric, I'm calling on everyone who calls themselves My friend, and I'm saying, 'I have a son over in Liberia. I'll give you the coordinates, I'll supply you the airfare, I'll provide you with everything you will need for the task, but I need you to get to him and be a father to him.'"

It was as if God were saying, "I am looking for a man who is willing to feel what I am feeling, one who is willing to go and do that which I would go and do if I were there on Earth. I am not there, except through you. I am a father to the fatherless in and through you. Remember, you are My body."

(For a powerful message based upon this story, watch the short film "Depraved Indifference" at www.ellerslie.com.)

That experience revolutionized our perspective on sacrificial love. We recognized that we could not rely on mere human capacity to love and care for the weak the way that Jesus does; we needed a supernatural impartation of His very heart. We asked for a love that would no longer say, "I will go this far, but no further," but rather, "I will give up my life to rescue even one of the least of these."

We began to study what we like to call Christian heroism—the lives of men and women who spilled their blood for the weak, not out of duty or obligation, but as an expression of the Love that dwelled within them. And we asked for the courage to follow in their steps, by God's grace.

I still feel a long way from the inspiring lives of people like William and Catherine Booth, Elizabeth Fry, Amy Carmichael, Corrie ten Boom, and Gladys Aylward. But their examples of laying down their lives for the helpless continue to call me to greater depths of sacrificial love.

When Jesus rescued us, it was not easy or convenient. It required far more discomfort and pain than we could possibly imagine. And when we become His hands and feet to the weak, we may get "dirty in the trenches" and suffer pain, just as He did.

A SHIFT OF FOCUS

Catherine Booth wrote, "It will be a happy day for England when Christian ladies transfer their sympathies from poodles and terriers to destitute and starving children."[2] She reminded women that living for pleasure and filling their days with eating, drinking, dressing, and sightseeing left no time to serve God and become His hands and feet to the poor and outcast. We as modern Christian women can greatly benefit from this reminder as well.

Throughout this book we have talked about turning away from empty pursuits and pop-culture distractions. But once we forsake these things, what should we be doing with our time? In addition to cultivating our relationship with Jesus Christ and serving the people He has placed in our lives (husband, children, family members, friends), we have also been commissioned to rescue and defend the weak and vulnerable. This is not a special call for certain Christians. It's the by-product of coming away with Jesus. This is what Jesus Himself does. Listen to how He described the ministry that the Father sent Him to do: "He has anointed Me to preach the gospel to the poor; He has sent Me to heal the brokenhearted, to proclaim liberty to the captives and recovery of sight to the blind, to set at liberty those who are oppressed" (Lk. 4:18). And then He told us, "As the Father has sent Me, I also send you" (Jn. 20:21). What a sacred calling He has entrusted to us! Are we taking it seriously?

Hudson Taylor once made a convicting statement that certainly applies to American Christians today: "It will not do to say that you have no special call to go to [the mission field]. With . . . the command of the Lord Jesus to go and preach the gospel to every creature, you need rather to ascertain whether you have a special call to stay at home."

While God may not ask you to live in a foreign country, all of us are called to adopt a missionary mind-set no matter where God has placed us. Ask Him to show you where and how to start being His hands and feet to the weak. Though the need around the world is staggering, He often wants to cultivate sacrificial love within us by starting with one.

When Eric and I first began to feel the call of God to reach the orphans of the world, the idea was daunting. We didn't know where to begin. And then we heard about a baby girl from South Korea who had been abandoned because she had deformities on her feet and no fingers on her hands. And we knew this was the one God wanted us to start with. Today, this little girl is our daughter Harper Grace. Just over a year later, He led us to adopt a baby boy domestically and build a relationship with his birth mom through open adoption. As I write this book, we are in the process of bringing home two toddlers from Haiti.

God might not call you to adopt, as He has us. There are countless ways He may lead you to lay down selfish pursuits in exchange for a life of sacrificial love. The first step is willingness. The second is prayer. If you surrender your body, your life, your time, and your resources to His purposes, you can be sure that He will open your eyes to the ways in which He desires you to become His hands and feet. Here is a quick list of some of the people for whom God's heart is especially burdened:

- The persecuted church
- The fatherless and widows
- The impoverished

- Prisoners and slaves
- The sick and the elderly
- Refugees and foreigners
- The unborn
- The unsaved

Ask God to show you which of these areas to invest your time and energies into. It may be a combination of more than one. Ask Him to burden you with His heart and His love for these precious lives. And ask Him to open your eyes to the needs right around you and around the world.

MAKING THE EXCHANGE

If you are ready to turn away from a life built around selfish pursuits and temporal pleasures and embrace a life of sacrificial love, here are some practical ways to begin.

1. BE A *Christian*, NOT A HUMANITARIAN

In recent decades, liberal thinkers both in and out of the church have hijacked the concept of standing up on behalf of the weak. Gospel-centered rescue work has been replaced by humanitarianism. While at first glance the idea of humanitarian aid might seem positive, it is opposite of God's message. Just take a look at this definition of *humanitarianism* from dictionary.com:

the doctrine that *humanity's* obligations are concerned
    wholly with the welfare of the human race
the doctrine that humankind may become perfect
    without divine aid (emphasis added)

The idea behind being a humanitarian is to showcase the good side of humanity and to celebrate our human ability to make the world a better place without God's help or involvement. It has nothing to do with the glory of God, and everything to do with the glory of man. If you are a humanitarian, you are not rescuing the weak as an extension of God's sacrificial love toward the world. Rather, you are serving and rescuing in order to proclaim, "Look at the good we humans are capable of!" That is why so many celebrities and icons have taken up humanitarian causes. They look to humanitarian acts to somehow prove that they are "doing their part" in this world and to convince themselves that they are spending time on worthy causes.

While there is nothing wrong with many acts of humanitarianism, such as feeding the hungry and creating fair-trade work opportunities for the impoverished, humanitarianism cannot provide the true solution to the world's problems. Why? Because it seeks to provide a solution outside of God.

Contrary to popular belief, what this suffering world needs is not primarily food distribution programs or fair-trade employment opportunities. The true solution is Jesus Christ. The hope and transformation that the Gospel brings offers the only permanent solution to the problem of human suffering, both in this life and in the life to come.

That is not to say we should preach the Gospel without ministering to people's physical needs. Rather, the two must go hand in hand. The book of James says, "If a brother or sister is naked and destitute of daily food, and one of you says to them, 'Depart in peace, be warmed and filled,' but you do not give them the things which are needed for the body, what does it profit? Thus also faith by itself, if it does not have works, is dead" (2:15-17).

The Gospel is both spiritual and practical. We can't just preach to others about Jesus; we must also do the works that Jesus did. But as we tend to people's physical needs, we must not overlook their much deeper need for salvation of the soul. Faith without works is pointless, but works without faith is just as meaningless. It is like putting a Band-Aid over skin cancer; it might cover up the problem, but it doesn't heal the problem.

Probably no other Christian organization in history has ministered to the needs of the poor like the Salvation Army. In 1865, William and Catherine Booth began their ministry by sharing the hope of the Gospel with some of the most hopeless and destitute people in London's East End. When these people experienced the transforming power of Jesus Christ, a profound change took place in them, not just in their spiritual lives, but in their daily conduct. Men who had been squandering their money on alcohol, causing their wives and children to starve, began to provide for their families. Women forsook lifestyles of prostitution and crime.

The Booths and their fellow Christian officers also ministered to the practical needs of the poor—offering job opportunities for men coming out of prison, food for hungry children, and housing for displaced women. But those forms of ministry were merely an outflow of their primary mission: bringing the salvation of Jesus Christ to the poor and destitute. Because they lived out a Gospel that was rich in both works *and* faith, the Salvation Army succeeded in putting a significant dent in the problem of poverty all around the world. (For an inspiring look at how the powerful work of the Salvation Army began and grew, I recommend the documentary entitled *Our People*. It is a great illustration of the distinction between Christian rescue work and humanitarianism.)

It is time for us to reclaim the Gospel-centered rescue opportunities that God has waiting for us all around the world. Don't let humanitarians redefine what it means to "make the world a better place." The only way to improve this world is to introduce it to true Christianity. As you are taking steps toward living an outward-focused life, don't be enticed by save-the-world strategies that bypass Jesus Christ. Any cause that you take up should flow from your desire to become Christ's hands and feet to this lost and dying world, and to bring glory to *His* name, not as a tribute to humanity's goodness. (For more on this subject, I recommend the messages "The Gospel Worldview" and "Of Pink Ribbons and a Bloody Cross," available for free download at www.ellerslie.com.)

2. VENTURE OUT OF YOUR *Comfort Zone*

I will never forget the day when Hudson, at age three, learned what an orphan was. A close family friend had just returned from a trip to Haiti where she had visited an orphanage and taken heartbreaking photos of children in desperate need of loving homes. As a wide-eyed three-year-old, Hudson stared at the pictures of the forlorn and sickly kids. He asked, "Who dose kids? Why dey sad?"

I explained that the children in the photos were orphans. Hudson asked, "What's an orphan?" I gave him the best definition I could think of: "An orphan is a child who doesn't have a mommy or daddy to take care of him." Stunned, Hudson said nothing. It had never occurred to him that somewhere in the world there were children without parents to take care of them. When I told him that there were lots and lots of orphans, he was even more perplexed and disturbed.

A few days later, after giving the matter some serious thought, Hudson came to me with a proposal: "Hey, Mommy, know what? If we bring dose kids in our family, dey won't be orphans anymore."

Without realizing it, my three-year-old had just enunciated God's solution for the orphan crisis around the world (see Ps. 68:5-6). Hudson was convinced that he had a perfectly good Mommy and Daddy, so why not share them with kids who didn't have any parents to care for them?

He went on to propose that we go to Haiti and adopt twenty orphans. I smiled at his childish enthusiasm and then informed him that I didn't think we'd have enough room in our house for twenty children. "Where would they all sleep?" I asked him. Hudson didn't have a ready reply, but a few days later, he came bounding down the stairs and told Eric and me he needed to show us something. We walked to the upper level of our house and discovered that Hudson had created orphan beds all around our house. Each orphan bed consisted of a blanket, a pillow, and one of his favorite stuffed animals. There were two orphan beds in Mommy and Daddy's room, one or two in the hallway, a couple in Harper's room, and about five in Hudson's bedroom. (He'd taken the greatest burden of caring for these orphans upon himself!)

"See?" he exclaimed. "We *do* have room!"

Eric and I were speechless and teary eyed. *If it were only that simple*, I remember thinking to myself.

But in reality, it *is* that simple.

When children see the orphan crisis, they quickly grasp the solution: Share what you have with those in need. Open your home, your heart, and your life to vulnerable children. Love them sacrificially. Even if you have to lose a bit of your comfort to do so, and even if it means sharing your favorite stuffed animals with them.

It is relatively easy for us to toss money toward an orphanage fund, or to send toys and gifts to impoverished children during the holidays. Those small acts are needed and important. But God has called us to more. He doesn't ask us to stand for the weak every once in a while, whenever it's easy and convenient. Rather, we are called to a lifestyle of serving them. This will look different for each of us.

Some of us may be called to minister to the homeless; others to adopt; others to fight for the unborn; others to start orphanages overseas; others to encourage the persecuted— and hundreds of other possibilities. Allow God to stretch you beyond what is comfortable and easy. We as Christian women usually have full lives, and often we believe we don't have much time or energy available to serve those in need. But we must remember that what God calls us to do, He equips us to do.

If you study the lives of Christian women who have made the most impact for God's kingdom, you will notice that it was rarely, if ever, convenient for them to do what they did. Their mighty acts for God required enormous personal sacrifice and a willingness to venture far beyond the realm of the easy and comfortable. If today's Christians are too busy, who will take up the torch of Gospel-centered rescue work in *this* generation?

Of course, serving the weak is not the only thing that we are supposed to do in this life. God entrusts us with many other callings, such as loving our husbands, training our children, ministering to the Body of Christ, practicing hospitality, encouraging younger women, being diligent in our places of work, and so on. And we are not to neglect our families or the other things God has called us to in order to serve the weak.

So how do we do all these things and still embrace a lifestyle of sacrificial serving? Here are some suggestions.

Involve your kids. It's easy to see the child-raising years as a season built around soccer practice, playdates, homework help, and piano lessons. While these developmental activities are important, we are called to train our kids to be ambassadors of the Gospel of Christ. That means teaching them to turn outward, to get outside their comfort zones and to love sacrificially.

Ask God to show you ways that you can get your kids involved in turning outward and serving the weak. Even if your children are young, you can still find ways to help them to be Christ's hands and feet to the weak. As a family, we study the needs of the persecuted church around the world (The Voice of the Martyrs and persecution.org are great resources), and our kids send letters of encouragement to pastors imprisoned for their faith. We are currently working on planning a family trip to visit and encourage families of persecuted Christians. All four of our children have been involved in preparing our home for the two toddlers we are soon to adopt from Haiti. They pray for their new siblings daily and even use their own money to purchase special gifts for them. When some friends of ours brought their older adopted boy home from Haiti, our kids made welcome signs for him and left special gifts in his bedroom.

The first time we visited our soon-to-be adopted children in Haiti, we brought Hudson along. He was seven years old. Seeing the needs and destitution of an impoverished nation firsthand made an incredible impact upon him and gave him a vision for doing something bigger with his life than just playing with Legos. He sponsors a little boy in Haiti and prays for his sponsored child daily. He writes him letters and sends him special gifts. Hudson has also come up with several fund-raising ideas for orphans in Haiti since that time. We frequently speak to our kids about the needs of orphans around the world, and they constantly talk about rescuing orphans when they grow up. As our kids get older, we have plans to take them to various places around the world where they can experience what it means to become Christ's hands and feet to the needy and vulnerable.

Even if you are a mom with young kids at home, remember that there are still many ways you can be Christ's hands and feet to the weak. In fact, you have an amazing opportunity to demonstrate a lifestyle of sacrificial love to your kids by teaching them about the needs around the world and helping them become part of the true solution.

Work together with the Body. Remember that you don't have to take on the problems of the world by yourself. If you feel burdened about a specific area of need, talk to other like-minded women you know about joining forces. Meet to pray for God's direction as to how you can work together to make an impact. Find out what other ministries already exist in these areas, and look for ways to come alongside them and serve what they are doing, or look through their websites for ideas and practical steps your group can take. For example, The Voice of the Martyrs outlines some practical ways to pray for and encourage the persecuted church. Christian Alliance for Orphans and FamilyLife offer many great resources for getting involved in orphan care. Compassion International provides opportunities to change a child's life through sponsorship, and Samaritan's Purse provides ways to get involved serving the impoverished. These are just a few among many great Christian service-oriented ministries that exist. Even many local churches have established ministries to orphans, widows, refugees, prisoners, the elderly, and so on. Look for ways to join up with others in the Body who are passionate about the burdens upon God's heart.

Remember that "changing the world for Christ" often starts with small first steps. But be sure that the ones you take are stretching you as far as God wants to take you! Be willing to venture outside the range of what is comfortable for you. Each step of sacrificial love will expand your capacity to take on even bigger burdens for the kingdom of God.

3. FIGHT THE *Right Battles*

"Going green" is one of biggest trends in our society right now. You can't walk out your front door without seeing green dry cleaners, green gas stations, green baby formula, or green toothpaste. Using catchphrases such as "preserving the earth's natural resources" or "cruelty-free" is a sure way to make any company seem modern, enlightened, and culturally relevant.

On the flip side, admitting that you forgot to recycle is like confessing that you are a convicted criminal. Failing to celebrate Earth Day with your children makes you an irresponsible parent. And using disposable diapers instead of cloth means you value your own convenience above the fate of this planet.

Raising awareness for endangered animals or aspiring to

become a marine biologist and rescue the whales may seem caring, responsible, and even spiritual (especially among postmoderns). But as we've been discussing, God has bigger, more important battles for you to fight. Despite what modern "greenies" may believe, this earth is not our home. God's heroes throughout the ages have lived not as long-term residents of this planet, but as mere pilgrims passing through (see Heb. 11:13,16). First Peter 2:11 reminds us that we are to be "aliens and strangers" in this world, not seeking an earthly home, but a heavenly one (NASB).

Of course, during the time we are temporarily here on this earth, we should take care of what God has given us. There is no reason to trash and pollute the planet or disregard the lives of animals just because our true citizenship is in heaven. Christians who act this way are only living selfishly and failing to represent the nature of Christ. But when we invest major efforts into trying to save and preserve this earth, and stress over things like global warming, we are focusing on what is temporal and not eternal. God says that we are to set our minds on things above, not on earthly things (see Col. 3:2).

Environmentalists dream of maintaining the earth for thousands of generations to come, because they believe this earth is their long-term residence. They believe that this is the only home we and every future generation will ever know, and thus it is our responsibility to make it last as long as possible. But Jesus says that His kingdom is not of this world (see Jn. 18:36). John 3:16 does not say, "For God so loved the *earth*" (meaning the trees, soil, and animals on this planet) but rather, "For

God so loved the *world*" (meaning the lost *human souls* on this planet). Jesus gave His life to rescue lost humanity, not to preserve the earth's natural resources or save endangered animals.

In Romans 1, Paul warns against worshiping and serving the creature rather than the Creator. When we begin to worship and serve the things on this earth, we fall into the trap of idolatry and we turn the Truth of God into a lie (see Ro. 1:25).

As children of God, we are called to build and promote His kingdom. As you choose which causes to spend your time and energy on, evaluate what God is truly passionate about—saving the planet or saving souls. While it's fine to recycle or take steps to prevent animal cruelty, don't devote your life to such causes. God is in the business of delivering justice and mercy, setting captives free, bringing health to the sick, clearing the debts of the poor, and breaking the shackles of slavery. He burns with fury when He sees the weak and the little ones being exploited. He cries with indignation when He sees child prostitution in Cambodia, abortion in America, death squads murdering street children in Brazil, and little boys and girls struggling to live in a garbage dump in Central America. Most of all, His heart breaks for the hundreds of thousands of souls that die each day destined for eternal separation from Him.

These are the life-or-death battles He has called us to fight.

Eric wrote the following comments about becoming a Christian hero:

Our God is not passive, and He is certainly not unfeeling. He has entrusted His children here on earth with the job of expressing His indignation, His compassion, His generosity, and His love here in this physical world. Christians are supposed to be His hands, His feet, His voice, and His response to these atrocities in the natural realm. If it appears God is doing nothing to halt these horrors, the blame for inactivity falls squarely on the shoulders of those of us entrusted to be His representatives. It's Christians that bear the onus of culpability. We are the ones commissioned to carry out God's epic agenda, and if we fritter our lives away pursuing puny goals and do nothing to stop these horrors, then we will stand before God in the end with a stain of responsibility upon our souls.

As you evaluate where to devote your time and energy, remember that rescuing human lives and souls is true kingdom work; saving whales and trees is not (see Jas. 1:27).

During the Jewish Holocaust, a certain church building in Germany was situated near some railroad tracks. Each week, cattle cars carrying trainloads of Jews would rattle by the church on their way to the death camps. The Jewish prisoners could see the church through cracks in the sides of the cattle cars. "If anyone will help us, it will be the Christians," they said. So they screamed as loudly as they could, begging the churchgoers to do something to help them. Inside the church building, the Christians grew uncomfortable. They didn't want to listen to the anguished cries of those Jews. They didn't want to get involved. If they did, they might end up on one of those cattle cars too. So they sang their hymns as loudly as they could, to drown out the cries of the suffering humanity only a few yards away.[3]

Oh, may we not be guilty of the same selfishness and hardness of heart. There are cries of anguish resounding all over the world—from the starving child to the Christian being tortured for his faith. May we not drown them out with our movies, T.V. shows, social lives, and career pursuits. God is asking each of us to turn down the volume of our own loud singing and learn to give the way He gave, holding nothing back.

LET'S TALK ABOUT IT

Group Study and Discussion

1. READ JAMES 1:27 AND JAMES 2:15-17. What kind of sacrificial love has God called us to? Why is this a crucial part of the Gospel?

2. READ MATTHEW 25:31-46. Why is it crucial that we exchange selfish pursuits for an outward-focused lifestyle? What is the difference between doing this out of obligation versus as an outflow of our love for Christ?

TAKE IT DEEPER

Personal Study and Reflection

READ: PROVERBS 31:20

REFLECT: Have I been living selfishly? Do I feel God calling me to a lifestyle of sacrificial love? What are some practical steps I can begin to take in this area? Am I willing to get out of my comfort zone in order to do this?

READ: ISAIAH 58:6-7

REFLECT: In what ways do I feel God is asking me to reach out to the weak and vulnerable on His behalf? How can I become His hands and feet to this lost and dying world?

Making Your Choice

IT IS TIME TO MAKE YOUR CHOICE.

You are standing between two kingdoms—one a thriving land of ease, pleasure, and comfort; the other a humble, hidden hole in the side of a mountain. One promises acceptance, distraction, and pleasure. The other promises persecution, difficulty . . . and true fulfillment.

Can you hear that gentle voice calling your name? It is the voice of the one true King, saying:

> *I have chosen you. I have called you by name. I ask you to come away from Saul's camp and become numbered among My set-apart ones who dwell with Me in the cave. Bring nothing with you, leave everything behind, and do not look back. Cut off all allegiance to your former homeland, and come away with Me. It will not be an easy path. But unless you die with Me, you will never know what it means to truly live. Come away to the cave. Come away with your King.*

The King has called you by name. He has chosen you to be counted among His faithful ones, a set-apart woman after His own heart.

It is time to make your choice. Are you ready to say yes to His sacred invitation? Will you join the host of set-apart women throughout history who have chosen to live by the following creed?

> I have decided to follow Jesus,
> I have decided to follow Jesus,
> I have decided to follow Jesus—
> No turning back, no turning back.
>
> The world behind me, the cross before me,
> The world behind me, the cross before me,
> The world behind me, the cross before me—
> No turning back, no turning back.
>
> Though none go with me, I still will follow,
> Though none go with me, I still will follow,
> Though none go with me, I still will follow—
> No turning back, no turning back.*

*Inspired by an Indian Christian in the 1800s who boldly spoke these words in the face of death, as he and his family were martyred for their faith in Christ. After their heroic deaths, their killers were so moved by the family's courage and faith that they too became Christians.[1]

Recommended Resources

THE FOLLOWING IS a list of books that have greatly impacted me in my journey toward becoming a Christ-centered woman. If you are looking for messages that will freshly ignite your spiritual passion and deepen your faith in Christ, this list is a great place to start!

STORIES OF GREAT CHRISTIANS

Gladys Aylward: The Little Woman by Gladys Aylward with Christine Hunter

Gold Cord: The Story of a Fellowship by Amy Carmichael

Of Whom the World Was Not Worthy by Marie Chapian

Great Women of the Christian Faith by Edith Deen

They Found the Secret: 20 Transformed Lives That Reveal a Touch of Eternity by V. Raymond Edman

A Chance to Die: The Life and Legacy of Amy Carmichael by Elisabeth Elliot

Shadow of the Almighty: The Life and Testament of Jim Elliot by Elisabeth Elliot

Through Gates of Splendor by Elisabeth Elliot

These Are the Generations by Eric Foley

No Compromise: The Life Story of Keith Green by Melody Green and David Hazard

C. T. Studd: Cricketer & Pioneer by Norman Grubb

Rees Howells: Intercessor by Norman Grubb

If I Perish by Esther Ahn Kim

George Müller of Bristol: His Life of Prayer and Faith by A. T. Pierson

Chasing the Dragon: One Woman's Struggle Against the Darkness of Hong Kong's Drug Dens by Jackie Pullinger

A Retrospect by James Hudson Taylor

Hudson Taylor's Spiritual Secret by Dr. and Mrs. Howard Taylor

The Hiding Place by Corrie ten Boom with John and Elizabeth Sherrill

Tramp for the Lord by Corrie ten Boom with Jamie Buckingham

The Cross and the Switchblade by David Wilkerson with John and Elizabeth Sherrill

The Pastor's Wife by Sabina Wurmbrand

Hearts of Fire: Eight Women in the Underground Church and Their Stories of Costly Faith by The Voice of the Martyrs

BOOKS TO STRENGTHEN YOUR RELATIONSHIP WITH CHRIST

The Cost of Discipleship by Dietrich Bonhoeffer

Power Through Prayer by E. M. Bounds

Purpose in Prayer by E. M. Bounds

The Pilgrim's Progress by John Bunyan

God's Missionary by Amy Carmichael

If by Amy Carmichael

The Seeking Heart by François Fénelon

Foxe's Book of Martyrs by John Foxe

The Christian in Complete Armour by William Gurnall

The Power of the Spirit by William Law

Mere Christianity by C. S. Lewis

The Screwtape Letters by C. S. Lewis

The Complete Works of Oswald Chambers with notes by David McCasland

Abide in Christ by Andrew Murray

Absolute Surrender by Andrew Murray

An Apostle's Inner Life by Andrew Murray

With Christ in the School of Prayer by Andrew Murray

The Scottish Chiefs by Jane Porter

Why Revival Tarries by Leonard Ravenhill

Revival Praying: An Urgent and Powerful Message for the Family of Christ by Leonard Ravenhill

The School of Christ by T. Austin-Sparks

The Treasury of David by Charles Spurgeon

In the Footprints of the Lamb by G. Steinberger

The Mystery of Godliness by Major W. Ian Thomas
The Saving Life of Christ by Major W. Ian Thomas
The Power of Prayer by R. A. Torrey
The Pursuit of God by A. W. Tozer
God's Pursuit of Man by A. W. Tozer
The Knowledge of the Holy by A. W. Tozer
Of God and Men by A. W. Tozer
God Tells the Man Who Cares: God Speaks to Those Who Take Time to Listen
    by A. W. Tozer

Notes

CHAPTER ONE: THE DIVINE INVITATION

1. Charles Spurgeon, "A Sermon for Spring," No. 436, February 23, 1862, http://www.ccel.org/ccel/spurgeon/sermons08.x.html.

CHAPTER TWO: CLINGING TO THE CROSS

1. Amy Carmichael, *God's Missionary* (Fort Washington, PA: CLC Publications, 2010), 34.
2. Catherine Booth, *Aggressive Christianity: Practical Sermons* (Philadelphia: National Publishing Association for the Promotion of Holiness, 1883), 32.
3. Leslie Ludy, *Set-Apart Femininity* (Eugene, OR: Harvest House, 2008), 31–33.
4. Helen H. Lemmel, "The Heavenly Vision," 1922, public domain.
5. Evan Hopkins, *The Law of Liberty in the Spiritual Life* (London: Marshall Brothers, 1884), 127–128.
6. Andrew Bonar, *Memoir and Remains of the Rev. Robert Murray McCheyne* (London: W Middleton, 1845), 21.
7. Adoniram Judson Gordon, *How Christ Came to the Church, the Pastor's Dream: A Spiritual Autobiography* (Philadelphia: American Baptist Publication Society, 1895), 14.
8. Jackie Pullinger, "God Uses Foolish Things," http://www.sermonindex.net /modules/mydownloads/singlefile.php?lid=18861&commentView=item Comments.
9. Amy Carmichael, *Gold Cord: The Story of a Fellowship* (London: Society for Promoting Christian Knowledge, 1952), 58.
10. George Bennard, "The Old Rugged Cross," 1912 (public domain).

CHAPTER THREE: AWAKE, MY SOUL

1. A. W. Tozer, *God's Pursuit of Man* (Camp Hill, PA: Wingspread, 2007), 5.
2. Elisabeth Elliot, *Discipline: The Glad Surrender* (Grand Rapids, MI: Revell, 2006), 104.

3. E. G. Carré, *Praying Hyde: Apostle of Prayer: The Life Story of John Hyde* (Alachua, FL: Bridge-Logos, 2004), 129.

4. Leonard Ravenhill, *Why Revival Tarries* (Minneapolis, MN: Bethany House, 2004), 85.

CHAPTER FOUR: REDEEMING THE TIME

1. John Tauler, quoted in Amy Carmichael, *God's Missionary* (Fort Washington, PA: CLC Publications, 2010), 39.

2. Leonard Ravenhill, quoted at https://www.goodreads.com/author/quotes /159020.Leonard_Ravenhill.

3. David Wilkerson, *The Cross and the Switchblade* (New York, NY: Berkley, 1977).

4. *Strong's Concordance*, s.v. *kenophónia*, http://biblehub.com/greek/2757.htm.

5. *Blue Letter Bible*, s.v. *oikodomē*, http://www.blueletterbible.org/lang/lexicon /lexicon.cfm?Strongs=G3619&t=KJV.

CHAPTER SIX: HE MUST INCREASE

1. Jackie Pullinger, *Chasing the Dragon* (Ventura, CA: Regal, 2006), 102.

2. Amy Carmichael, *If* (Fort Washington, PA: CLC Publications, 2011), 30–31.

3. Amy Carmichael, *Gold Cord* (Fort Washington, PA: CLC Publications, 1991), 57.

4. Ian Thomas, *The Mystery of Godliness* (Grand Rapids, MI: Zondervan, 1964), 162.

5. C. H. Spurgeon, "The Lily among Thorns," No. 1525, February 29, 1880, http://www.spurgeongems.org/vols25-27/chs1525.pdf.

6. Gerard Manley Hopkins, "To What Serves Mortal Beauty."

7. Elise Moreau, "What Is a Selfie?" About Technology, http://webtrends .about.com/od/Mobile-Web-Beginner/a/What-Is-A-Selfie.htm (accessed 8/13/2014).

8. "Purely and Simply a Sister," *Set-Apart Girl*, July 31, 2014, http://setapartgirl .com/magazine/article/07-31-14/purely-and-simply-sister.

CHAPTER SEVEN: AN UNDIVIDED HEART

1. The Voice of the Martyrs, *Hearts of Fire* (Nashville, TN: W Publishing Group, 2003), 109–110.

2. The Voice of the Martyrs, 109–157.

3. Interview with Leonard Ravenhill, Redpath/Ravenhill interviews originally broadcast on *Chapel of the Air*, http://ia700809.us.archive.org/18/items /SERMONINDEX_SID0776/SID0776.mp3.

4. Rachel Jankovic, *Loving the Little Years: Motherhood in the Trenches* (Moscow, ID: Canon Press, 2010), 58–59.

5. Esther Ahn Kim, *If I Perish* (Chicago, IL: Moody, 1977), 30–32.

6. Corrie ten Boom with Jamie Buckingham, *Tramp for the Lord* (New York: Jove Books, 1978), 159–160.

7. Leslie Ludy, *Sacred Singleness* (Eugene, OR: Harvest House, 2009), 68.

8. Norman Grubb, *C. T. Studd: Cricketer & Pioneer* (Fort Washington, PA: CLC Publications, 2008), 60.

9. Grubb, 61.

10. Grubb, 61–62.

11. Leonard Ravenhill, http://ia601200.us.archive.org/22/items/SERMON INDEX_SID1375/SID1375.mp3.

CHAPTER EIGHT: THE SOLID ROCK

1. Elisabeth Elliot, *Quest for Love* (Grand Rapids, MI: Revell, 2002), 35.

2. Henry Ward Beecher, *Life Thoughts* (London: James Blackwood and Co., 1858), 119.

3. dc Talk and The Voice of the Martyrs, *Jesus Freaks: Stories of Those Who Stood for Jesus* (Tulsa, OK: Albury Publishing, 1999), 35–36.

CHAPTER NINE: STRONG AND COURAGEOUS

1. Gladys Aylward with Christine Hunter, *The Little Woman* (Chicago: Moody, 1970), 29–30.

2. Corrie ten Boom with John and Elizabeth Sherrill, *The Hiding Place* (Peabody, MA: Hendrickson, 2009), 32.

3. Elisabeth Elliot, *Discipline: The Glad Surrender* (Grand Rapids, MI: Revell, 2006), 101.

4. Thomas Chisholm, "Great Is Thy Faithfulness," 1923 (public domain).

CHAPTER TEN: SO I SEND YOU

1. Norman Grubb, *Rees Howells: Intercessor* (Fort Washington, PA: CLC Publications, 2008), 93.

2. Frederick St. George de Lautour Booth Tucker, *The Life of Catherine Booth: The Mother of the Salvation Army, Volume 1* (New York: Revell, 1872), 474.

3. Penny Lea, "Sing a Little Louder," http://www.internationalwallofprayer .org/A-010-Holocaust-Memorial-Day-Stover.html.

EPILOGUE: MAKING YOUR CHOICE

1. "I Have Decided to Follow Jesus," http://www.hymnary.org/text/i_have _decided_to_follow_jesus.